IT'S A LIVING

© 2013
Text copyright: Gerard Sasges
Image copyright: Mai Huyền Chi

Published by:
Ridge Books
an imprint of NUS Press
National University of Singapore
AS3-01-02, 3 Arts Link
Singapore 117569
Fax: (65) 6774-0652
E-mail: nusbooks@nus.edu.sg
Website: http://www.nus.edu.sg/nuspress

ISBN 978-9971-69-698-6 (paper)

National Library Board, Singapore Cataloguing-in-Publication Data
It's a living : work and life in Vietnam today / edited by Gerard Sasges. – Singapore
:¬ NUS Press,¬ 2013.
pages cm
ISBN : 978-9971-69-698-6

    1. Vietnam – Social conditions. 2. Vietnam – Economic conditions..
    3. Vietnam – Social life and customs. I. Sasges, Gerard.

HM51
301.09597 -- dc23   OCN840448531

Designed and typeset by: Mai Huyền Chi
Photographs by: Mai Huyền Chi
Printed by: Tien Wah Press Pte Ltd

IT'S A LIVING
work and life
in Vietnam today

edited by
Gerard Sasges

images by
Mai Huyền Chi

with a foreword by
Andrew X. Pham

NUS PRESS · SINGAPORE

FOREWORD

Fourteen years ago, I met a young man at a UC Berkeley social event for visiting academics from Vietnam. I can't recall the academics, the other guests, or the many animated discussions, but I remember very clearly one intent young man named Gerard Sasges.

We had a brief chat. He was working on his dissertation, but he was also searching for a sense of meaning and purpose in life. Cloistered academia had begun to wear. He talked to me because I had just taken a year-long solo bicycle trip and written about it in a book, and was about to launch headlong into another journey.

It was easy to urge a man down a path his heart already yearned for, even easier when one had been down a similar road and enjoyed it immensely. I often thought of it as standing on a mountain top next to a bicyclist, who is staring down a long, steep descent on an unfamiliar single dirt track strewn with boulders and unseen twists and turns, urging him forward with a gentle nudge and the words "Yes, yes, you can always come back and pick up where you left off."

Alas, it is but a minor deception, inconsequential in the greater scheme of "knowing how way leads onto way." Such is the fate of beginners. I once scribbled a few lines a long time ago as a very young man contemplating his first voyage:

Why do we go?
Because we are afraid.
Then why don't we stay?
Because our cowardice might diminish us.
What do we fear?
The malice of strangers. Inconveniences.
Mysterious ends of unmarked roads.
Will the act of departure define us?

I know the answer now: Yes, always, irrevocably.

When Gerard contacted me recently, he explained "It's actually thanks to your advice that I stayed in graduate school, went to Vietnam, finished my PhD, and ended up spending more than ten years living and teaching in Hanoi." I find it very rewarding to know that others have benefited from my work and words. As most writers know, monetary compensation, even awards don't amount to much on the greater scale of things. They say you can't take it with you, and it's true. But I bet that if there's anything you can take beyond this existence, it's the karma you've earned from the positive impact you've had on the lives of others.

And that's what I believe Gerard and his students have achieved with their book, It's a Living, an ambitious compilation and translation of interviews with ordinary Vietnamese about their lives and occupations. The premise of the book is beguiling in simplicity, but its content is epic in scope, cutting a clean slice from the Vietnamese social economic strata from top to bottom. The sheer variety of interviews and the ringing honesty of the interviewees' words make for an impressive and revealing read. The translation is clean and uncluttered. Reading it in English, I can hear clearly their voices speaking in Viet. This is the sign of a first rate translation.

A year or two in a country does not make an expert out of anyone. A decade does. Ten years of immersion in a place, of joys, sorrows, discoveries, heartbreaks, friendships, anger, despair, and hope. In that time — a full quarter of an adult human's working life — a man will have lived, loved, and lost, not once but several times. And if he has the eyes willing to see, the heart willing to feel, the mind willing to understand, then and only then does he becomes an expert. That's what Gerard has invested in Vietnam, and it shows. It's a Living is, without a doubt, the best non-fiction work on Vietnam I've seen in a decade.

San Francisco, April 2013
Andrew X. Pham

PREFACE

The interviews in this book were conducted as part of a class I taught while directing the University of California's Education Abroad Program in Vietnam. I'd come to Vietnam in 2000 to begin research for a PhD in History at the University of California at Berkeley. Two years later, I was appointed the local director of the UC program, a position I enjoyed so much that I didn't give it up until ten years later. Although the program was originally designed for American students, over the years I gradually integrated local students into my classes so that by 2008, I was guiding equal numbers of students from the US and Vietnam as we investigated the processes of change we call "development." By 2010, I had decided to organize our investigations around the theme of work, and Project Kiếm ăn was born. As we explained on the project website,

> Translated literally from Vietnamese, "kiếm ăn" means "forage" or "look for food." In addition to describing what every living creature does to survive, it's also a slang term for working. By using this term, we want to emphasize that no matter what the outward form, every occupation shares the same basic concern of making a living. That means that the people we interview as part of this project are not just CEOs and factory managers. They're garbage pickers and mobile phone saleswomen, advertising executives and sex workers, motorbike parkers and rice farmers, promotion girls and drug dealers. All of the interviews are intended to help us develop a better understanding of the reality of working in Vietnam today, and through that, a

*better understanding of the reality of living in a
period of incredible change in the nation's economy,
society, and culture.*

Over the course of two years, we conducted more than 150
interviews, and made many of them available on our website in both
English and Vietnamese. The present book brings together selected
interviews from Project Kiếm ăn with images by my student and
friend Mai Huyền Chi.

We drew our inspiration for the project from many sources. In
the 1920s and 30s, Vietnam went through an earlier period of rapid
economic growth and urbanization that in many ways prefigured
the processes of change we see in Vietnam today. One result was a
social realism movement in Vietnamese literature that saw authors
like Vũ Đình Chí and Vũ Trọng Phụng produce wonderful works
of reportage introducing readers to the worlds of rickshaw pullers,
sex workers, and household servants, among others. Closer in time
but not in space, the 2000 book *Gig: Americans Talk About their
Jobs* reminded us of the incredible range of occupations that lurk
beneath the surface of contemporary societies, and the monologue
style of its interviews provided a model for our own editing process.
Like these works, our project was shaped by two ideas. First is the
notion that our work is an important window on ourselves and our
world: it's what we do to survive, and most human beings will spend
the greater part of their waking lives doing it. The second is the
idea that every job, and every person doing that job, is worthy of our
respect, our interest, and our time.

Some of the people we interviewed we knew already, some of
them were introduced to us by friends or family, and others we
just met by chance. Interviews usually, but not always, involved at
least two interviewers. Before we began, we prepared ourselves by
learning something about the job and discussing our strategies. As
part of the project, we had developed a shared template of questions
and themes to investigate, but we were also conscious of the need to

allow each conversation to take its own course. As much as possible, we tried to engage in a dialogue with people: we explained who we were, where we were from, and what we were trying to achieve, and we encouraged them to ask questions of us, too. Some people gave us permission to make an audio recording, but more usually they did not, in which case, we either took notes while we were interviewing, or we recreated the content of the session immediately after it was over.

For those of you who have done research in Vietnam, you'll know that the standards of informed consent required of professional anthropological research in the West are difficult to attain in Vietnam. Asking people to sign a typical consent form would have rendered many of our conversations impossible, and would have changed the nature of any we were still able to do. Within these limitations, however, we did our best to create conditions of informed consent. We explained our project to everyone we talked with, we let them know that our work might be published, and we gave them the opportunity not to participate, to participate anonymously, or to review the text of the interview before publication.

Interviews were first transcribed from the audio recordings and notes, then edited and translated as needed. The first step of the process was taking out the questions, then changing the order or removing parts we felt were repetitive. Our goal was to capture the flavor and ideas of the original conversation, but in a format that was accessible and engaging to the average reader. We then translated the text into English or Vietnamese. In general, we placed our interviews toward the colloquial English side of the spectrum on the logic that we wanted the language to sound as natural and appropriate in English as it did in Vietnamese. Most of the original translations were done by the interviewers themselves; some, though, I've done myself. For all of them, I bear final responsibility for any mistakes, deformations, or omissions that may have occurred in the editing or translation process. For interested readers, many of the interviews are available in Vietnamese on the project website.

In most interviews, we've changed the names and enough details to make it difficult to identify the people we talked with. Particularly in Vietnam, it can be hard to anticipate all the possible contexts where information might be considered sensitive, so it seemed best to err on the side of caution rather than unintentionally expose our informants to any negative repercussions. It will be obvious, though, that with some interviews — for example a company director or a well-known artist — it was impossible to avoid identifying the person. In these cases, they've given us permission to use their real names.

Some readers may be surprised at the way the interviews are organized. While the basic arc of the narrative, beginning with a rice farmer and ending with a bone cleaner, may have a certain logic, the journey between them takes some twists and turns. This is deliberate. My goal was to juxtapose certain occupations we might not normally associate with each other and to call into question assumptions about their relative value to society. After all, both an artist and an art forger are producing goods for the market, and a homemaker may have to solve problems as complex as any faced by the director of strategy for a multimillion dollar confectionary company. A prison inmate is as much part of the systems that keep a nation safe as the men and women who guard its borders. The point of contrasts like these is to underline the way all of us are engaged in the same basic enterprise: making a living.

Singapore, 2013
Gerard Sasges

ACKNOWLEDGEMENTS

This book would not have been possible without the people who took time out of their day to sit down with us and talk about their jobs. Our first debt of gratitude, then, is to all the people we interviewed between 2010 and 2011. Next, I'd like to thank all the students of EAP Vietnam and the UCHANU class. Whether they participated directly as contributors or indirectly through their enthusiasm and inspiration over the years, they're all a part of this project. Special thanks go to the irrepressible Ali Wong, a participant in that first and epic EAP semester, who gave me her dog-eared copy of *Gig* and unknowingly started the ball rolling back in 2002. I also have to thank everyone at the UC EAP offices who placed such trust in me and provided me with unfailing support over the years: especially Peter, Mary, Nicole, Joyce, Eva, Doris, Inés, Amy, and May.

I'm also indebted to our wonderful collaborators at Hanoi University, particularly Trương Văn Khôi, Hoàng Hương Giang, and Hoàng Gia Thư. And I really cannot thank enough my superb program coordinators, Phạm Thị Phương Liên and Nguyễn Thu Trang, and my student, colleague, and brother Alex-Thái Đình Võ.

Finally, I'd like to dedicate this book to the millions of working women and men of Vietnam who get out of bed in the morning — or work through the night — to make a living for themselves and their families. Without them and the millions of different jobs they do, the crazy beautiful place that is Vietnam would not be possible.

CONTENTS

CONTRIBUTORS

Conceived and edited by
Gerard Sasges

Images and design by
Mai Huyền Chi

Foreword by
Andrew X. Pham

Interviews contributed by
Son Chau, Micaela Bacon, Lena Tran, Nguyễn Hương Lan, Nguyễn Phương Vân, Vi Le, Katie Do, Emily Shaw, Đào Duy Khương, Đinh Xuân Phương, Lan Ngo, Jeremy De Nieva, Nguyễn Thị Thao, Nguyễn Thúy Linh, Tina Ngo, Peter Del Moral, Đoàn Hồng Hải, Nguyễn Hải Yến, Kathy Nguyen, Andrew Marvin, Đỗ Thu Hiền, Đoàn Lê Thoa, Kristine Nguyen, Mary Luc, Jesse Van Fleet, Đinh Hà Thu, Nguyễn Phương Chi, Mai Nguyen, Carol Nguyen, John Tran, Trương Minh Giang, Đỗ Thu Hương, Thu Nguyen, Nancy Pham, Đào Tuấn Dũng, Nguyễn Hồng Ngân, Eliza Tran, Jennifer Phung, Nguyễn Minh Dương, Lỗ Thị Lan Anh, Irene Van, Sharon Seegers, Vũ Hoàng An, Nguyễn Thái Linh, Minh Thu Diep, Sean Decker, Phạm Phương Thảo, Huỳnh Đình Quang Minh, Thuy Mai, Hae Jin Kang, Bùi Phương Thảo, Nguyễn Thị Thu Huyền, Colleen Ngo, Josh Mayhew, Mai Lan, Mai Quang Huy, Ngoc-Diep Tang, Haven Rocha, Hoàng Huyền Trang, Vũ Phương Thảo, Lena Tran, Maya Weir, Nguyễn Thùy Trang, Vũ Thu Hiền, Chieu-An Ton Nu, Peter Le, Lê Phương Linh, Đỗ Đăng Tiến, Tina Bao-Ngan Ngo, Annelisa Luong, Nguyễn Thị Lan, Bùi Hà Phương, Mai Nguyen, Loc Le, Hoàng Minh Trang, Nguyễn Huy Anh, Tracy Nguyen, Đinh Đoàn Vũ, Nguyễn Thanh Nga, Trương Công Tuấn, Michelle Ta, Tina Thy Pham, Ngô Mai Hương, Nguyễn Hà Phương Ninh, Tuan Tran, Mai Huyền Chi, and Gerard Sasges.

NOTE TO THE READER

About Tết: References to Tết, the Lunar New Year, appear in dozens of the interviews that follow. Tết is the most important holiday in the Vietnamese calendar, and is often described as a sort of Thanksgiving, New Year, and birthday all rolled into one. Lasting up to a week or more, it is a time for families and friends to come together through parties, celebrations and ceremonies often centered on the family's ancestral village.

About place names: In 1976, Saigon, the former capital of the Republic of Vietnam, was merged with the surrounding province of Gia Định and officially renamed Ho Chi Minh City. Today both names are commonly used in Vietnam. In this book, I use "Ho Chi Minh City" to refer to the metropolitan area, and "Saigon" to refer to the city's historical core centered in District One.

About prices. At the time we did the interviews, the exchange rate for the Vietnamese đồng was hovering at just over 20,000 đồng to 1 USD, which is the rate I've used to give US dollar equivalents. It's also worth noting that inflation was upwards of 10 per cent per year, which means that even in the relatively short period we did the interviews there were appreciable changes in prices and salaries.

About orthography: Vietnamese words that are commonly used in English, like "Vietnam," "Hanoi," "Saigon," or "Ho Chi Minh City" have been written following English practice; all others use Vietnamese diacritics. As for personal names, I've used English orthography and order for everyone from the United States, and standard Vietnamese for people living in Vietnam.

INTRODUCTION

One of my favorite taxi rides in Vietnam took place in late 2008. Once the driver and I had gone through the usual details of age, family status and the like, I steered the conversation in the direction of work: how long he'd been driving a cab, working hours, income in an average month, the details that went to make up an ordinary day. The driver described how he had previously worked in a state-owned factory that had closed in the 1990s. After that, he'd gotten his license and driven trucks long-distance before switching to taxis five years before. Driving a taxi was stressful and the salary low, but combined with his wife's income, it gave him and his family a lifestyle that would have been unimaginable when he'd worked for the state-owned factory. "You know," he said, "the economic development Vietnam has seen since 1986 is thanks to the free market, thanks to competition, thanks to consumers being free to choose from a range of products. If Vietnam is going to keep on developing, this country needs to have a free market in politics, not just economics." His eyes, framed in the rearview mirror, sought out my own. "Do you understand what I mean?" he asked deliberately. "Yes," I replied, "I understand what you mean."

There are many reasons I like this conversation. It shows how even the most mundane conversation can reflect the sweep of Vietnam's recent history: Đổi Mới [market-oriented reforms beginning in the early 1980s] and painful economic restructuring, followed by new opportunities, growth, and real improvements in material welfare. It illustrates the nature of "market Leninism," where the Vietnamese Communist Party has given up much of its control over the economy while still retaining its monopoly on political power. And it hints at the increasing willingness of ordinary Vietnamese to criticize the Party and its policies as rising inflation and economic slowdown after 2008 eroded much of its claim to legitimacy. All of this from a few questions about how someone came to drive a taxi for a living.

I first arrived in Vietnam in the summer of 2000. As I began to learn the language in the months that followed, my conversation partners were the tea ladies, market vendors, and motorcycle taxi drivers who were a part of my everyday. And of all the possible starting points for a conversation, work was inevitably the most engaging. After all, how can we not have something to say about what we do for most of our waking hours? As time went on, however, I came to understand that these exchanges were more than simply a means of passing the time or practicing my Vietnamese. They provided a window on how people were living incredible processes of change at a particular moment in Vietnam's history, yet simultaneously revealed experiences and values that resonate across time and space to speak to all of us.

For Vietnam, the end of the Second World War ushered in a long and devastating period of conflict that at different times and in different places involved elements of anticolonial struggle, social and economic revolution, civil war, ethnic strife, and Cold War geopolitics. Estimates vary, but somewhere between 2 and 3 million Vietnamese lost their lives in the Indochinese Wars that followed; today the conflicts live on in the bodies and memories of the survivors, and in an environment scarred by the use of millions of tons of bombs, ordnance, and toxic chemical defoliants. For most of the people we interviewed these struggles are something they learn about through the media or in history textbooks, but for others they are much more real. Among the accounts that follow, an elderly calligrapher recalls his wartime career as an interpreter for Soviet technicians. A Catholic statue craftsman remembers life on the collectivized farm and policies intended to eradicate "superstitious practices." A retired nurse struggles to describe the experience of arriving at the scene of an aerial bombing raid.

On April 30, 1975, the surrender of the US-backed Republic of Vietnam and the reunification of a country divided for more than 20 years brought only a tenuous and temporary kind of peace. Those labeled supporters of the former regime faced lengthy terms in harsh reeducation camps, followed by exclusion from the centrally planned economy. Southern Vietnam's large ethnic Chinese community, long prominent in commerce and industry, first bore the brunt of policies that forcibly collectivized private property, then found themselves victims of rising tensions between Vietnam and its former ally, China. In December 1978, Vietnamese troops invaded Cambodia, toppling Pol Pot and his brutal Khmer Rouge regime; the following February saw Chinese troops mount a short but destructive invasion across Vietnam's northern border. While the Chinese soon withdrew, Vietnamese troops would remain in Cambodia for another 11 years fighting a grinding guerilla war against the remnants of the Khmer Rouge and their allies.

With the ongoing war in Cambodia, a US-led embargo crippling international trade, and output from the collectivized farming system dropping, for many people, the years of peace that followed reunification in 1975 brought disappointment, hunger, fear, and a desperate struggle for survival. Hundreds of thousands of Vietnamese, like our moving service operator, fought in Cambodia or in the war with China; over a million more chose to leave the country, braving government patrols, sharks, storms and pirates in what became known as the "boat people" exodus. Today, they make up a large part of the more than 2.5 million Vietnamese living abroad. Their stories are also part of the larger story of the nation, and thus the following pages include a number of interviews of overseas Vietnamese.

By the early 1980s, the defects of the centrally planned economy had become impossible to ignore, and a series of reforms — driven as much by local realities as central directives — saw market elements slowly introduced into the command economy. This process deepened and accelerated after the 1986 Party Congress, officially ushering in the Đổi Mới period of "market-oriented socialism" that continues to this day. For a short while, new economic freedoms were accompanied by a flowering of political participation and criticism. But by 1989, events in Eastern Europe and China had strengthened the position of those who saw in these political freedoms a potential threat to the Communist Party's monopoly on power. While the last decades have seen the Party relax many of the formerly strict controls over society, today Vietnam remains a single-party state with an efficient and active security apparatus, where those who engage in public forms of dissent face harassment, arrest, and imprisonment.

The economic reforms after 1986 combined with increasing integration into the global marketplace for goods and services to transform Vietnam's economy and society. Not all the transformations have been easy. The 1990s saw thousands of inefficient State Owned Enterprises [SOEs] restructured or closed and hundreds of thousands of workers, like our flower seller, forced to find new, less stable forms of employment. The dependence on production for export has opened up new opportunities but at the same time exposed farmers and workers directly to the vagaries of a global marketplace. New foreign-invested factories have created new jobs, but less participatory forms of labor organization and management have contributed to unrest visible in the thousands of strikes — officially illegal but generally tolerated — that have occurred since 2000.

Nevertheless, the overall effect of these transformations has been to bring real material benefits to the lives of ordinary Vietnamese. The gradual dismantling of the collective farm system and the introduction of private land rights after 1986 contributed to a rapid increase in agricultural production; after years of near famine, Vietnam was once again an exporter of rice by the late 1980s. The withdrawal of Vietnamese troops from Cambodia in 1989 was followed by the normalization of trade relations, first with Europe and then with the United States. This process of integration accelerated still further in 2006 when Vietnam became a member of the World Trade Organization. Throughout the 1990s and early 2000s, real GDP growth hovered around 6 per cent annually. Even more striking, according to government figures, was the way the same period saw the percentage of the population living in poverty drop from over 60 per cent to less than 15 per cent. By 2009, GDP per capita was over $1,100 and the World Bank had ranked Vietnam a "lower middle income" country, seemingly confirming its status as a shining example of successful economic development.

The global economic crisis after 2007 may have exposed some of the limits of development in Vietnam. Despite years of growth, the economy has remained unable to escape its dependence on cheap labor and low value-added products. Rapid growth has overwhelmed much of the nation's infrastructure and exacted a heavy toll on the environment. Endemic corruption means Vietnamese from every walk of life face an unending stream of exactions both large and small; when combined with economic mismanagement, it has resulted in billions of dollars wasted or diverted to economically unproductive ends, seen most famously in the effective collapse of the state-owned Vinashin corporation in 2010. Finally, as Rolls Royces jostle with bicycles on the crowded streets of Hanoi and Saigon, the unequal distribution of the nation's newfound wealth acts as a brake on development and places increased stress on Vietnam's social fabric.

By the time these interviews were conducted in 2010 and 2011, that social fabric had already been weakened by decades of policies that owed less to socialist orthodoxy than to the global neoliberal consensus. Crucial services such as health and education had been opened up to private competition and the remaining state sector subjected to rising user fees. The goal of these policies, described somewhat euphemistically as "socialization," was to shift costs from the state to the individual. For those with means, the policies brought impressive improvements in the range and quality of services available. Yet those without were made increasingly vulnerable to illness, accident, and the rising costs of basic goods and services. Thus when annual inflation rates began pushing into the double digits at the end of the decade, many Vietnamese saw their standards of living erode for the first time in recent memory. For some, the experience called into question key features of an economic, social, environmental, and political contract that had held largely unchallenged since 1990.

However this contract may evolve in the years ahead, it has already served to transform the lives of Vietnamese people. One of the most striking developments has been the transformation of the landscape. For many in the countryside, the combination of rising prices and rising expectations means that farming — the traditional backbone of the economy — can no longer provide a living. As our butcher asks, "If everything depended on a few sào of rice fields then how in the world would we have enough to eat?" One response has been to seek supplementary sources of income, whether staying in the village or through temporary migration. Others have responded by leaving the countryside more permanently, only returning for planting or harvesting, or to celebrate Tết. Another factor driving the rural-urban transition is shifting land use. Across Vietnam, huge swathes of agricultural land are being turned into industrial parks, housing developments, multi lane highways, and golf courses, with opaque processes of land appropriation and allocation often sparking protests and other forms of struggle. Looking around her at the village's ever-shrinking fields, our rice farmer wonders where Vietnamese will get their rice from when all the farmland is gone.

Whether or not her imagined future becomes a reality, it's impossible to deny that for more and more Vietnamese, the landscape has become a cityscape where rural rhythms are replaced by an urban cacophony. Vietnam's urban population is growing by approximately one million people annually, with the populations of the two largest centers, Ho Chi Minh City and Hanoi, each over 7 million. For many, the city means new opportunities for employment, education, entertainment, and consumption. Our young multilevel marketer, for example, sees the city as a bright and shining place of almost limitless potential. Yet for others like our scale lady, the city is a tiny space in a rooming house and lonely days spent walking a maze of cold, alienating streets. As she says, "I'm alone all the time, I walk the streets alone, I wait for customers alone. Customers come, pay money, and leave without talking to me. It's a sad job but what else is there to do?"

As the previous paragraphs suggest, migration — whether temporary or permanent, from the countryside to the city, or even from Vietnam to abroad — is driven by a complex interaction of pulls and pushes. But almost inevitably, decisions to leave the quê nhà ["home place": a deeply affective concept in Vietnamese involving notions of place, ancestors, history and identity] are motivated in large part by a sense of obligation to family. Parents move in search of better schools for their children and the money to pay for university tuition. Children move for better jobs and the means to provide for their parents in old age. These webs of obligations are incredibly strong, expressed linguistically in such concepts as ơn [debt] and hiếu [filial piety], and financially in the sums flowing across spaces and generations both within Vietnam and across its borders. At the level of the individual, it can take the form of the $50 a shoe shiner in the city sends home to his wife each month; aggregated it can take the form of the more than $8 billion in remittances to Vietnam from abroad each year. Yet at the base of both figures is family. As our laundromat owner, eking out a living in her new American home, says, "I'm happy and I keep working because I want my family to be okay. Sure we'll always have to struggle, but we came all the way to America for this kind of life." Her sentiment echoes in dozens of the interviews that follow.

Notions of family and place thus remain central to Vietnamese identity. Nevertheless, it's important to acknowledge the ways in which society and culture are changing under the influence of increased exposure to a global market in goods and ideas. Cơm bình dân ["rice of the common people"] restaurants are being supplanted by KFC and Pizza Hut. Local television stations broadcast the latest Korean dramas. Young Vietnamese listen to hip-hop music and practice their breakdance moves. Ho Chi Minh City has its own professional basketball team, the Saigon Heat, cheered on by their very own Saigon Hotgirls. And while for many of the people we interviewed, the Lunar New Year celebrations remain a crucially important time to reconnect with family, friends, and their quê nhà, for others it is a time of boredom and lost business revenue.

Perhaps nowhere are these changes more apparent than in the realm of marriage, sexuality, and gender. Young urban women particularly are delaying marriage and defying the convention to marry by their late twenties. For those men and women who do marry, divorce is increasingly common, with divorce rates rising 50 per cent in just five years after 2005. Similarly, premarital sex, previously taboo, is increasingly common. As our hotel receptionist says of his many teenage clients, "It seemed like they were already pretty used to going to hotels." And as his comment implies, the meaning of sex is changing. Our adult store salesperson may have never seen a condom before she began working, but now she and her customers are well acquainted with the latest toys, appliances, and other aids their parents probably never dreamed existed.

The increasing pervasiveness of market relations has had powerful effects on gender and gender roles. Our homemaker feels an obvious need to defend her decision to forego work outside the home, and interviews ranging from a factory line worker to a highly paid executive point to the active roles millions of Vietnamese women play in this new economy. This economy makes heavier demands on some women than on others, however. Fragmentary glimpses of Vietnam's pervasive sex industry, ranging from women "selling flowers" on the street to cắt tóc ôm ["hug hair salons"] to exclusive karaoke bars, appear in many of our interviews. Taken together, these glimpses provide a particularly clear example of the way women can be commodified: the girls in a karaoke bar, after all, are known not by their name but by their number.

Yet the story is more complex than simple commodification. Explaining why her job entails more than looking pretty, our young PG ["Promotion Girl"] points without apparent irony to the physical demands of working long shifts in an air-conditioned environment standing in stiletto heels and a tiny skirt. But for her, this objectification is voluntary, temporary, and limited. She sees being a PG as part of her education, along with her university degree providing the skills, confidence, and connections she'll need for an eventual career in management. While the new flexible, market-oriented economy may have brought with it new forms of commodification and served to erode the kinds of formal gender equality that characterized pre-Đổi Mới Vietnam, for many women the last decades have also brought mobility, opportunity, and economic independence.

The last decades have also brought change for Vietnam's LGBT community. The manager of a long-standing gay bar in Hanoi describes how the mix of customers has changed over the years: originally made up almost entirely of foreigners, her customers today are predominantly Vietnamese. Straight herself, she talks of her many gay friends and describes her customers as being "like family." Yet when asked how she would feel if her child were homosexual, she pauses before replying, "Nobody wants their child to be that way." Nevertheless, with legislation recognizing same-sex marriage set to be debated in the National Assembly in 2014, it's clear that gender norms, like so many other aspects of economy, society, and culture in Vietnam today, are changing rapidly.

The interplay of change and continuity is thus one of two

important threads linking the stories that follow. The second one that emerges from our interviews is the experience and the meaning of work. For many people, work is simply a way of making a living. As our motorbike mechanic explains, when he first started as an apprentice, he loved his work; now, though, he loves the money more. Perhaps the most telling account in the collection belongs to a young bank employee. Despite excellent working conditions and a high salary, she laments the systematization and grinding monotony of her job and regrets the loss of her carefree youth, all at the age of 24. Money and status, she has learned, is no guarantee of happiness. Nevertheless, she stays, trapped by the combination of high salary and social pressure.

Yet for many others, work has a deeper meaning. Reading their stories, it's hard not to be struck by the satisfaction that people derive from knowing their labor is going to provide for their loved ones. It's also hard not to be struck by the sense of craft, pride, and even joy that many people find in their work. While you might expect to hear these sorts of sentiments expressed by a film director or a well-known artist, it often resonates most clearly in the words of a knife sharpener, a bus ticket collector, or an electric appliance repairman. This latter, for example, is so passionate about his work that for him, paradise would be incomplete if it didn't come with appliances to fix. His words are a powerful reminder that work can be much more than just a way to make a living, and that paradise is where we find it.

chapter 1

GROWING

farmer

How long have I been a farmer? I've been working in the fields
since I was 18; I'm 48 now so I guess that's 30 years. I learned the
skills from my family, from listening to the village's community
loudspeaker system and from personal experience. Farming is
passed down through generations, so I suppose a farmer is meant
to follow the career path of their parents. My parents were farmers,
so I'm one too [*laughs*].

An ordinary day working in the fields is hard. It starts at 6 a.m.
This job isn't like a factory job or anything like that, so the hours
aren't fixed. This job is very inconsistent. When it's harvest season,
I may have to work from morning until noon, take a quick lunch,
and then continue working until 7 or even 8 p.m. But if it's not
harvest season, it's leisurely. We don't have to go to the fields and
housework isn't hard. Farming follows the seasons of the year.

These days, farmers have to know how to combine different
jobs. After all, there are only two rice crops per year. In between
the rice seasons, farmers have to grow other crops like vegetables
and flowers. For example, right now, we're growing Vietnamese

water spinach. In the other off-season we might grow kohlrabi or cabbage. If we grow vegetables as well, we can double or even triple our income. Everybody does it, everybody has to, or else we'd die of hunger [*laughs*]. And when I'm not farming, I run a business buying and selling recyclable materials. Between all my jobs, I have to work every day of the month. There's no such thing as a 'day off'. There are two rice crops per year, and when I'm not growing rice, I'm growing vegetables. And when I'm not growing crops, I'm in my shop buying and selling recyclables. At night, I work until about 8 p.m., eat dinner, and go to sleep. What do you mean, what do I do for entertainment? Sometimes I watch a little TV to relax; that's it.

Things used to be different. Back in '81, when I graduated from high school, I went right into the cooperative, even became the secretary for the local branch of the Youth Union. During the harvest season, there were a lot of pests like chafer beetles and moths. We'd catch them by taking a lantern like this one [*indicates a lantern hanging in the shop*], and putting it in a big tub of water that we'd place out in the fields at night. Every house was responsible for buying at least three or four lanterns; I can't even remember how many we had. At night, there would be so many of these moths, and when they saw the lantern, they would flutter around and around the light until they got exhausted and fell into the tub of water below. Then we'd collect them and bring them to the cooperative office. That's how we did it back before we had the "modern" methods we use today [she uses the term "scientific," the reference is to pesticides and herbicides]. It was a lot of fun, and young people like me were called upon to play a leading role. Every household — husbands, wives, and kids — would all go out and catch moths. It was fun back then, it was fun.

It was the same with collecting insects in the fields. When we were harvesting rice, if we came across plants that were infested with insect nests, we'd collect those too. With 200 — or maybe it was 20 nests, you know, I can't even remember — we would get a kilo of paddy [unhusked rice]. Because at that time, the value of everything was calculated in paddy, you see? Then at the end of the year, the management would calculate how much each member of the cooperative had earned. At that time, I'd never worked for pay in my life, so you can imagine how surprised I was when all those insect nests I'd collected turned out to equal 50,000 đồng [$2.50] at the end of the year. Today, of course, that's nothing, but back then it was enough to buy a bicycle. A bicycle, can you imagine? So I took the money that I'd earned from the insect nests, brought it to my mamma and said, "Look at all the money I got for us, mamma; it's for you" [she uses the familiar terms of address "u" and "em"]. And you know what she said? She said, "No honey, it's your money. You take it and get yourself a bicycle." Now remember, I'd never made a cent before in my life; my folks never had any money, we had to make everything we needed ourselves. And so that's how I got a bicycle worth 50,000 đồng for the first time in my life [laughs]. The first time!

Sure, there's been progress since then. For example, plowing had to be done with buffaloes but now we have motorized tillers. In the future, rice fields will get smaller, and more and more land will be used for industry. When that day comes, there won't be any more farming. People like me will be old by then, but our kids' generation will still be young and they'll have to leave the village. Even if they didn't want to leave, there wouldn't be any fields for them to work. I guess it's better like this. But if the farmland keeps shrinking and the population keeps growing, how will we have enough food? Maybe scientists can develop a new kind of rice as big as a longan: just a few grains and you're full [laughs].

Has farming impacted me? Obviously! There's an old saying about people like me: "Farmers have to sell their face to the earth,

and their backs to the sky." And working the whole day long in the sun, in the UV rays, has definitely affected my health and my beauty [*laughs*]. But I've never been hurt on the job, I just get tired. And luckily I've never had any health problems. But at the end of the day, even though farming is a really low-paid job, we have to love our work: we don't have a choice. Vietnamese farmers just have to love their work; I mean really, what other jobs are out there? Maybe if I were younger, I could find another job, but at my age, there's really nothing else for me.

Gia Lâm, September 2010
Irene Van, Nguyễn Thái Linh, Sharon Seegers, Vũ Hoàng An

butcher

You can really say that in my life, I've had to take the bitter with the sweet and the sorrow with the joy. From a spiritual point of view, being a butcher is one of the worst professions possible, but still, people need meat and so society needs butchers. My dad would sometimes slaughter cows on the side; and so, to put food on our table and clothes on our back, I've made this profession my own for more than 20 years now. And being a cow butcher is no picnic: you're working till all hours of the night then getting up at the crack of dawn — always working like a dog.

Like most folks in the village, I'm just a simple hardworking farmer. But the money we make from farming a few sào [in Northern Vietnam one sào is 360 square meters] of rice fields just

isn't enough to live on, so at a certain point I decided to follow
in the footsteps of my dad, and of my grandfather before him.
Years back, when I was still a kid, my dad sometimes slaughtered
cows just like I do today. The difference is that there wasn't that
much demand back then; people mainly raised cows to use as draft
animals in the fields. I guess the profession of cow butcher is a
family tradition.

Sometimes it seems like everything about my work is done
backwards. During the day when everyone else goes to work, that's
when the rest of the family and I can actually take a rest because
we usually start work at midnight and then work till morning.
If we've got a lot of orders, we'll start earlier, say from 9 p.m. On
those days, we can kill anywhere from three to five cows. Then in
the morning, the customers will come and pick up their orders.
Sometimes, if people have cows they want to sell, they'll give me a
call and I'll come by to see what the animals are like. If they're in
good shape, we'll negotiate a price and I'll take the cows home to
raise for a few days until we slaughter them.

These days, the price of everything keeps rising and rising, and
beef is no exception. Some cows are bigger and some are smaller,
it depends on how folks raise them. A little cow might go for 10
to 15 million đồng [$500–$750]; if it's big or a really big one, it's
going to be around 20 million [$1000]. We source the majority
of our cows from people we already know, and then they pass the
word around that we're the ones to go to if you need a butcher.
That way if someone has a cow they want to sell, they get in touch
with me. Before, my wife had to take the meat to the market and
sell it herself because we didn't have enough regular customers
making orders yet. But over the years we've come to the point
we're at today: where "Lâm Nam the butcher" has become a kind
of trademark around here. As for competition, well, there really
isn't any to speak of because in the whole village there're only a few

families in this line of work. Each family has their customer base and that's just how it is.

Most folks going to the market never give a second thought to the process that turned a live cow into that nice cut of beef they're taking home for dinner. If they could actually see a cow being slaughtered, though, most of them would be disturbed, to say the least. That's the reason why I hesitated to let anyone interview me about my work. But given that you're from the village, that makes you almost like family, so I guess I'll just lay it out for you and hope it all turns out okay.

As you can imagine, having done this job for so long now, it's really become second nature. We do everything by hand, from the day I first started till now. First, I choose a healthy cow and then tie its legs to a pole. Then I take a sledgehammer to the nape of the cow's neck, or more precisely to the back of its head, and keep hitting it until it's dead. After that, I make an incision in the neck to drain and reserve its blood. Next, I slice the cow open from its chest down, skin it, and remove its intestines. Then the legs, the shoulders, and so on, until all that's left to do is wait for the customers to come and pick up their order. On average, the price of a kilo of rump these days would be about 130,000 [$6.50], round would be about 115,000 [$5.75], and flank only 85,000 to 90,000 [$4.25–$4.50]; it depends on the market at the time of course, but on average that's what it will cost you. And make no mistake, we use every part of the cow. The only thing left over is the half-digested food in its stomach, and even that we use for fertilizer.

Making a living isn't easy, and if everything depended on a few sào of rice fields then how in the world would we have enough to eat, pay our daily expenses, and send the kids to school? All we can do is keep working hard. My wife and I have six kids; of the six, the two older sisters have already gotten married, so that leaves their four brothers as my main source of labor, and let's not forget

their mother [*laughs*]! In the run-up to Tết, demand goes through the roof, what with all the customers buying meat to make giò, chả, and other traditional dishes. At that time of year there's no such thing as free time for me and the boys. We're working from seven at night until the sun comes up. On average, we butcher 10 to 15 cows a day, but that number can go as high as 20. If we work fast, one cow takes about 30 minutes, but a larger one can take up to an hour. Each person has their own specific roles, so we don't waste a second. For example, I handle the sledgehammer and drain the blood, my youngest boy skins the cow and carves the meat, and so on. Generally speaking, there are a lot of ceremonies and parties around the end of the year, so that's our busiest time of year. Otherwise, though, there's less work.

I've been doing this for a long time, so I can tell the quality of a cow just by looking at it. A cow with good firm flesh is almost always going to have been grass-fed. Cows that are fed grains or rice look completely different; their flesh is going to be fatty and it just won't taste as good. As for the income we can make, well, in general it's stable enough. I'll tell you straight, if I buy a cow for 15 million [$750], I'll make about 400,000 đồng [$20] in profit. Sometimes, though, I still end up making a loss. Let's say I buy some cows but don't slaughter them immediately because I don't get enough orders; well, then I've got to bear the cost of feeding them until I do. I can buy a cow at 100 kilos and in the course of a few days it can lose a dozen kilos. But this is just a regular part of the business. I remember once, I was bringing home some cows I'd bought when they stampeded and one of them was killed. I had to slaughter it as soon as I could get it home, but because we didn't have any orders yet my wife had to sell it for a loss at the market.

After doing this job for 20 years, I've got more than my fair share of memories, both happy and sad. I'll always remember one afternoon when I went to fill the weekly order of one of my regular customers. When I went to lead the cow out of the stables, it suddenly went crazy, pulled the lead out of my hands, and tried to charge me. No matter where I ran, it just kept charging at me, and I didn't want to run into the house for fear of the damage it could do as it tried to follow me. Then it occurred to me — use another cow to calm the first. And I'll be damned if it didn't work: as soon as we got that other cow out into the yard, the first one quieted right down and stood there peaceful as can be. In all these years I've only ever had that happen once. Sure, I can laugh at it now, but at the time it could just as easily turned out as tragedy rather than comedy.

If you want my opinion about the so-called "future" of this profession, I'd have to guess that my family will stick with it a long while more. But as for my kids, I want them to continue studying so that they can have better careers when they get out of school. The life of a butcher is a hard one, you're working to all hours of the night, then getting up at the crack of dawn.

Hải Phòng, September 2010
Đào Duy Khương, Vi Le, Đinh Xuân Phương, Katie Do, Emily Shaw

scrap food collector

I'm from Hưng Yên, near Gân market. I'm 39 years old and I'm married with two sons. My eldest son was born in 1997 and my youngest son was born in 2000. I guess you could say my family is happy. My wife and I are both farmers with limited education so our speech and actions might be a little rough sometimes. The good thing is that even if we both argue the night before, the next morning things are back to normal. We still do our work and life still goes on.

I got into the business of collecting scrap food through my wife. A few years ago, she got to know some restaurant owners while she was selling vegetables in Hanoi and offered to buy their scrap food for our pigs at home. The problem is my hometown in Hưng Yên has very few restaurants. They generally save their scrap food for themselves instead of selling it to outsiders.

The process of getting scrap food is really simple, but I've got to do it carefully and every day without fail or the restaurants won't save it for me the next time. On days that I can't go, I need to let them know so they can sell the scraps to other people or throw it away because it doesn't last until the next day.

Usually I leave the containers at the restaurants to be filled directly, then I switch them with empty ones the next day. Either that or I have to bring a big ladle to scoop the scraps from the restaurants' containers into mine. Most of my containers are 60 liters; some of them are recycled paint barrels. There are containers that are as big as 200 liters, but the amount of scrap food we need only fills up about two 60-liter containers and two paint barrels. I don't always get to fill up all of my containers every day, though.

My family raises about 40 pigs at home. The scrap food alone isn't enough food for them so I have to cook it together with corn and industrial rice bran. I drive the filled containers home

everyday, which usually takes about one hour, maybe a bit more.
I often get the scrap food from around the Hoàn Kiếm lake area,
then drive down Mã Mây street, and finish up at Chương Dương
bridge. Normally I go between 2 p.m. and 5 p.m. in the afternoon,
but I leave the house a bit later during the rice harvesting season.
I'll probably get home around 7 p.m. or 8 p.m. tonight.

Everybody in this profession gets their scraps from a different
place. Sometimes we meet each other to talk and have some iced
tea, but for the most part we aren't that familiar with one another.
Most scrap food collectors live in Hanoi, or in the suburbs from
Ái Mộ to Văn Giang along the levees. I live the furthest. In my
neighborhood, I'm the only one who travels to get their scraps
because of the distance involved, which is 20-odd kilometers.

I know I'm driving a big heavy motorcycle, so I try to drive
slower and closer to the side of the road. It's mostly men that do
this job: women can't drive as well so they really shouldn't drive
long distances carrying heavy things. You know the old proverb: a
weak water buffalo is better than a strong cow. I guess that makes
me the water buffalo [laughs].

Rainy weather is the worst to deal with. It makes driving so
much harder. Or other times, my motorbike has broken down
in the middle of the road while I'm collecting scrap food. The
motorbike breaks down quite often, usually because of a punctured
inner tube. There are days when I have to push the motorbike
loaded with scraps for almost an hour. Then there was one time
three years ago, when I was about a five kilometer drive away
from home, and a car crashed into me. The motorbike and all the
containers of food fell on top of me and I broke my leg. I couldn't
collect scraps for almost a year and my wife was forced to go in my
place. Not only that, we couldn't raise as many pigs. Fortunately,
my parents and brothers and sisters helped a lot with tending the
chickens and pigs while my wife was out. My leg is okay now but

it still hurts sometimes.

At the beginning, I was afraid of having to drive so far. Now I'm afraid of having to go every day. It's fine on days when I'm feeling good, but even on days when I don't feel well I still have to go or the restaurants will throw the scraps away. Plus I've already paid the restaurants up front. I spend about 600,000 đồng [$30] a month for the scraps, and another 600,000 on gas, so my total costs are a little over 1,200,000 đồng [$60] a month. Depending on the restaurant, I either pay the head chef or the owner directly. I raise my pigs for about six months until they're ready to be sold. The current market price for all the pigs I have right now is about 150 to 170 million đồng [$7,500–$8,500]. Raising pigs is like having money in the bank. Unfortunately, though, the rate of return is low.

In the morning, I feed the pigs and the chickens, then I go to work in the rice fields. At noon, if my sons come home from school early, they cook lunch for all of us. If they come back late, my wife or I will cook. After that I have an hour to take a short nap before I leave to go collect scrap food at around 2 p.m. I don't get back until five or six in the evening. Then I feed the pigs and chickens again. By the time I clean up and shower, it's nine or ten at night.

Farmers like us don't have that much free time. I just try to save some time for resting instead of going out drinking or gambling. And anyway, I don't have money to go out. My wife and I have been married for almost 20 years now, but we've never had the time or the money to take a vacation. Even during Tết I only take the first day off and work the rest. During the blue ear disease [Porcine reproductive and respiratory syndrome] epidemic a few years ago, the pigs didn't eat and they all died, but I still had to go collect scrap food. For two months straight I drove to Hanoi to collect scraps we couldn't use. We sold it to a fish farm when we could; otherwise we just had to throw the food away.

I'm already a manual laborer, plus I'm collecting a kind of garbage, so some people see this occupation as degrading. Generally, the restaurant owners treat me okay if they're understanding. But still, some people discriminate against me because my clothes are dirty and smelly. Sometimes I greet people, but they don't even bother responding. Other times, let's say if I accidentally create a small mess, people can get rude. I've encountered that a lot of times, but when it happens a few times at the same place, I try to find a restaurant where people are nicer.

This kind of work is exhausting, and of course I want to escape poverty. From 1999 to 2000, I tried to find opportunities to work abroad. There was this export labor company that said they could get me a job in Taiwan. I really wanted to get rich so I actually spent six months learning Chinese, then they told me to go home and wait. I actually gave them $3000 to arrange a contract for me. My wife and I had just gotten married a couple years before and we didn't have much savings so we had to borrow the money, mostly from my brothers and sisters. But I was really hopeful because everyone said I could make 5 or 6 million [$250–$300] a month working abroad. I waited for two years but nothing ever happened.

Then in 2002, they told me "you've done your passport, your personal profile is done, you don't need to study anymore, just go for an interview then it's done." I did like they told me to, but still nothing happened, so I gave up. Since then, I've convinced myself that going abroad isn't going to happen, and I just need to focus on working hard to pay off my debts. Luckily, we got through that difficult time. If I'd kept chasing that dream much longer, though, we might have lost all our land.

I know heaven has already decided my fate. I collect scrap food to decrease the cost of feeding my livestock a little. Frankly, I've got no love for this job. I only do it is because of circumstance. Of course everyone wants to eat delicious food, wear nice clothes, and have a nice clean office job, but I just have to accept that this is a part of my life. Everyone has to do whatever it takes to survive.

I tell my kids, "just look at your mom and dad, with no education, working day in and day out. That's why we pay for you to go to school so when you grow up you don't have to live like a poor farmer, so you can have an easy life." My kids may be young, but they understand the situation. My oldest is in ninth grade; he gets good grades every year. My wife wants them to concentrate on studying so we don't make them help out around the farm. It's okay if they want to do small chores like cook lunch, but we don't let them help with dinner because they have to study at night. And feeding the pigs is really hard work so we don't let them do that either. The pot of rice bran is huge, almost three times as big as a scrap food container — how are they going to carry it?

In the future, all the land in my village will be bought out by factories; no farmland means no more raising livestock. I'll be old by then so I'll just retire. I'll raise some chickens or plant a vegetable garden. My boys will grow up and go to the city for college and they'll escape this place. My wife and I can stay together in our hometown, and maybe when the boys come back to visit, they'll give us some money [*laughs*]. Actually, we've got a little money saved up, in case they want to open a business after they graduate. I know I can't collect scrap food forever. I'm getting weaker as I get older, so I know at some point I won't be able to keep this up. For now, I just focus on taking things day by day.

Hanoi, October 2011
Ngoc-Diep Tang, Hoàng Huyền Trang, Vũ Phương Thảo, Haven Rocha

bonsai grower

You see this tree here? I bought it for 8 million đồng [$400]. If I sell it now, I can get 600 million [$30,000]. If I wait another three years, I should get at least 7 trillion [$350,000]. See that other tree? It's almost 50 years old. I brought it home and transferred it onto that rock. It'll take three years until it's finished.

Basically, I find a beautiful old tree and hire someone to bring it back to my place. I go all over the country looking for trees I can work with: Thanh Hoá, Nghệ An, Phú Thọ, all over the North and the Center. Once I get it home, I take time to really understand its aesthetics. Friends and colleagues come around and look at it; the more perspectives I can get, the better. There's a saying, "If you've got nine people you'll have ten opinions." We're really open around here. We're not afraid of competition and everyone wants the other to do a good job. That's why I'm happy to talk to anyone who's interested in my trees; I can literally sit here and talk about trees for hours.

When you're growing bonsai, there are different seasons for doing different things. From January to August, you shape the tree by pruning and bending. From September to November, you promote growth by covering the tree with fabric or wrapping it in plastic. In December, it's too cold to do anything.

The bonsai industry started to develop in this village about five years ago. Many families are in the business now. I don't know exactly how it happened. I guess the younger people got together and decided it was a good job to have: not too dirty or physically demanding. At 47 years old, I'm actually the oldest person growing bonsai in the village. My master, Giang, is only 37. He's really skilled, and I've learned a lot from him.

So anyway, I grew up in the village, and after I got out of high school I went to work on the Red River for 16 or 17 years. It was

hard work and I had to be away from home a lot. Six or seven years ago, I started growing bonsai trees as a hobby, and gradually it turned into my profession.

I love this job. It's an art form and a kind of meditation at the same time. It teaches you patience and understanding and helps you become a more complete, civilized person. Sometimes I'm out here all night with one tree, trying to understand how I should work with it. Then other days when I'm not feeling inspired, I just sit here, drink some tea, smoke some thuốc lào [Vietnamese tobacco, smoked through a water pipe] and let my mind wander. In my previous job, I'd sometimes get frustrated or angry when something went wrong or I had to deal with jerks. But this job brings a clarity and lightness to my life. It's wonderful.

I don't need to advertise. Some people in the village have started advertising their trees online, and I'll probably do it too some day. But for now, people just hear about my trees by word of mouth. Pretty much anyone who's into bonsai will know about my trees and come visit. Sometimes they compliment and sometimes they criticize, but this job has taught me to be patient and accepting. Life is like that, I think. You have to be able to let things roll off your back and be at peace with yourself.

I'm old now. I have to admit I've been very lucky in my life. If you add up the value of all the trees here, it would be somewhere around 100 billion đồng [$5 million]. So I'm more than happy to make this my career. Not only do I get to work surrounded by all these beautiful trees, I can also expand the business so my kids can take over when they grow up. As the country develops and people become more cultured, demand for bonsai will only increase.

These trees are like my children. I love them all. You see that little bonsai over there? I raised it from a seedling and now it's eight years old. It's almost perfect now. If someone appreciates it, I'll be happy to sell it to them. But if not, I'm just as happy to watch it grow for the next 30 or 40 years. The more time and attention I invest in a bonsai, the more special it is to me.

Hồng Vân, November 2010
Nguyễn Thị Thao, Nguyễn Thúy Linh, Lan Ngo, Jeremy De Nieva

chapter 2
FEEDING

rice liquor maker

I've been making rice liquor since 1985. Even back when I was still working in construction, I was making rice liquor. I learned it from others, simply by following their instructions. It wasn't a job that got passed down in my family or anything like that. I was pretty bored after I retired, but then I got used to it. I keep busy by cooking liquor, doing housework, and looking after this little one right here [*points to her one-year-old grandson*]. It takes up my whole day! A typical day starts early in the morning. Each day I cook ten kilograms of rice, then I cook the liquor; just pot after pot.

For ingredients, I use unpolished rice; it's not the type of rice you normally eat at home. Either sticky or nonsticky rice works, but sticky rice produces sweeter and more aromatic liquor. Then there's yeast. For equipment, I use a big copper pan and a chicken intestine, a long copper pipe. When I'm distilling the liquor, it goes through the chicken intestine into a cooling reservoir, then into the bottle. You have to use a copper pipe because the steam from the boiling mash can melt plastic, which will make the liquor poisonous. Copper lasts longer and lets the liquor retain its taste and aroma. And over on that side are the basins and jars for letting the liquor sit and brew.

The first step is cooking the rice. It has to be cooked longer than the kind we normally eat but not as much as porridge. After cooking the rice, I spread it on a wide bamboo basket, wait for it to cool, and then put it in a basin. I alternate layers of yeast and rice. Then you have to wait for the mixture to go through the first stage of fermentation. In the summer, two or three days are enough. But if it's cold, it takes closer to five days. You can check by hand if it's ready or not — the mixture should be soft and there should be liquid in the basin. Next you put the fermented mixture in 10 to 15 big jars. You pour one and a half liters of water into the jar for each kilogram of rice. Then you cover it with a plastic or wooden panel so that the wine doesn't lose its flavor. Then you wait again — seven days if it's hot and up to ten days if it's cold. It's like wearing clothes: if it's hot, you wear just one layer, but if it's cold, you wear more. After that, you take the mixture out of the jar and distill it in the copper pan. When the mixture boils, the steam goes right into the "chicken intestine," through the cooling reservoir, and there you go — rice liquor!

Good wine should taste slightly sweet and burn a little — to tell you the truth, I don't even know how to drink it — but if it's sour, it's gone bad. Wine made from sticky rice tastes sweeter and smells better. It's funny how people get sick of eating just a bit of sticky rice, but they never get tired of drinking it! I only cook ten kilos of rice per day. I could cook more but we're tight on space; there's no room for more jars. Ten kilos of rice can produce seven or eight liters of wine — that's the strong kind — or ten liters of the weak kind.

To be honest, the whole process is hard work and takes a lot of effort. The most important part is cooking the rice and mixing it with the yeast. You can't make good wine out of overcooked or undercooked rice. Or when you let the wine sit and brew — it sours pretty easily in the summer. It ferments too quickly and goes sour. When that happens, I have to pour more water into the mixture and cook it again. The sour part goes to the bottom — you just throw that away — and take the top layer to sell. It's a waste of time and wine. Customers complain when the wine's gone sour; that happens mostly in the summer, but it's really pretty rare.

It's a hard job, but I've always had to work for a living, and I have to admit that having something to do every day keeps me from getting bored. Plus, I have a good reputation; people keep asking for my wine so I keep making it! It's pretty fun. I'd get bored otherwise, unsettled even, [*laughs and teases grandson*]. Grandma doesn't feel happy if she doesn't work!

Even though there're a lot more beer places and types of bottled liquor now, people are buying from me more than ever before [*laughs*]! [Daughter interjects: "We want to stop but people keep asking for it so we have to keep making it!"] People like the fact that my liquor is made pure and simple — it's not mixed with anything else — so they keep coming back. The liquor you find on the streets nowadays is made with Chinese yeast. With Chinese yeast, you don't even need to cook the rice, you just mix the yeast in with water and rice and wait two or three days. It doesn't go sour and you can get more liquor out of it, but it doesn't taste as good and it's bad for your health. I just stick to the old-fashioned way — always have, always will.

My customers buy directly from me and my family, not from restaurants or pubs. There's such a high demand that I can't fill all the orders sometimes. Some folks come all the way from Gia Lâm: that's 30 or 40 kilometers away! Some people come by every ten days and still can't get any liquor even after a month. I'd make more, it's just that there's no more space in my kitchen. I sell a liter for 40,000 đồng [$2] and make about 4 million [$200] in profit per month. Just enough money to put food on the table [*laughs*]! I could sell my liquor at a higher price, but I don't dare to because I have good relationships with all my customers. Raising my prices might create rifts.

I'll keep making liquor until I can't do it anymore [*laughs*]! I have three daughters: any of them can do this if they want, but I really don't think they want to. Making liquor requires a lot of space, time, and energy. You're inside all day. And truth be told, it may be something to do but it's not much to look forward to.

Hanoi, November 2011
Tina Bao-Ngan Ngo, Annelisa Luong, Nguyễn Thị Lan, Bùi Hà Phương

tào phở maker

My name is Liên and I'm 49 years old. I'm originally from Nam Định, but these days I live in Hanoi with my family. There are five of us, and we rent a house on Khương Trung Street near Đầm Hồng. As a mother, I'm really proud to be able to work and support my kids' dreams of pursuing higher education. All three of them are studying at different colleges. One of them is going to the Trade University, another is studying at the National Economics University, and the last one is going to the Water Resources University.

Before moving to Hanoi and selling tào phở [a soy-based, jelly-like dessert usually topped with ginger and syrup], I was a farmer back in Nam Định. I only had one or two paddy fields to make a living from. At the end of the day, it was all I could do just to feed my family — there was no such thing as "savings." If I was going to give my kids a better future, I knew I had to put them through school. So 15 years ago, I came to Hanoi and started selling tào phó. And thanks to this job, I've not only been able to feed my family, but also save money for my kids' education.

There isn't much to say about this job. One of the few changes I've noticed since I started is the price of a bowl of tào phó. When I first started, the normal price for a bowl was 500 đồng [2.5 cents]. But living standards keep rising and inflation rises along with them, so to keep up, these days I sell a bowl for 5000 đồng [25 cents]. This way, I can continue putting money aside for my kids. On an average day, I can make 250,000 đồng [$12.50]. After deducting 50,000 đồng [$2.50] for food to feed the family, and another 100,000 [$5] for the ingredients to make the tào phó, it means I save about 100,000 đồng [$5] each day. So in one month, I can put aside around 3 million đồng [$150]. There's no way I could make money like this back in Nam Định.

This kind of money doesn't come easy, though. Every day, I wake up at 12 a.m. to soak the soybeans. At 3 a.m., I start grinding and wringing the soybeans to make the tào phó. Then at 6 a.m., I take my bike out and start my day. Every morning, I start off at the Thanh Xuân market for a couple of hours. Then once I've sold the first tub of tào phó, I go home to get a new tub, and head back out again. By about 10:30 a.m., I drop by Hanoi University and sell there until I run out, which really depends on the weather. Because this job is so much work, I don't have enough energy to make and sell more than two tubs per day. Once I get home, I take a short nap. Watching TV, reading the newspaper, or going out are things that I just don't do. First, I don't have a TV, and second, I just don't have the energy. At 4 p.m., I start preparing dinner for

the family. After dinner, I clean up then head to bed. As you can imagine, your night ends early when your day starts at 12 a.m.

Selling tào phó may not look so hard, but you definitely have your share of problems. For example, in the past 15 years, I've been hit by motorbikes several times. Now of course I fall, my bike topples over, and all the tào phó is spilled. It's bad luck, but it can't make me give up. Or sometimes there are days when it just doesn't stop raining. On days like that, customers are few and far between, so all I can do is bring the leftover tào phó home, eat what we can, and throw the rest away, because tào phó is something that should never be saved for the next day. It spoils too fast, and no one wants spoiled tào phó.

There are also times where I would lose customers to other tào phó sellers, but that's not a big problem. I can always get my customers back by making my tào phó better and thicker, or simply by selling it at a cheaper price. My profits may go down, but at least I still have my customers. Fortunately, I don't have any competitors here at Hanoi University, and even outside the University when I do end up on the same street as another seller, we always know how to avoid each other.

One bad part about this job is the way city people tend to look at us with contempt. But the way I see it, even if they speak to us disrespectfully and make fun of us, it's not my problem. I enjoy my job, and I know that as long as I'm not cheating anyone, then no amount of scorn can change the value of who I am or what I do to make a living. Don't get me wrong, Hanoi also has many friendly, respectful people. These are the ones that I enjoy serving. These are the customers that keep a smile on my face through the day, especially when they speak to me and treat me like I'm family [a reference to the familial terms of address used in Vietnamese to denote respect or affection].

The friendly customers may be the reason I enjoy this job,

but it's always the thought of my kids that gives me the energy to continue working. Even though in my family, we have a tào phó recipe that's been passed on from generation to generation, I've still got no intention of passing this recipe on to my children. It's just not a good job to have; I don't want my kids to have to sell tào phó. They're more capable than that. So that's why all I want is for my kids to study, because an education will help them have a better job in the future.

I'm still young and I'm ready to continue at this job until my children have their own families, or as long as my body can handle this type of work. For now though, I'll just keep working hard, keep investing in my kids' success. These days, they are starting to be in a position to help me out financially, but I always refuse to accept their money. I know they need to pay for their education and other expenses; as a mother, nothing makes me happier than seeing my children grow, become independent and have a good job. I've never thought of them having to pay me back.

If I had the opportunity to do anything else, well, I wouldn't know what else to do. I've been selling tào phó for 15 years; I don't know anything else. But it's okay, because I'm motivated to keep doing this job for as long as it takes so my kids can get through school and start their own families. And who knows? Maybe someday soon, I'll be able to quit this job and stay home with my grandkids. As a matter of fact, one of my daughters just got married, so chances are I'll be able to retire soon [*laughs*].

Hanoi, September 2011
Chieu-An Ton Nu, Peter Le, Lê Phương Linh, Đỗ Đăng Tiến

chè maker

My name is Hoa, and I live in Bình Liêu town in Quảng Ninh. I
opened this chè stall in the town market almost ten years ago now
[chè is a sweet, soupy dessert, usually involving different kinds
of beans and jellies; it is eaten at almost any time of the day, and
particularly loved by children]. Sun or rain, winter or summer, 365
days a year, I'm here pretty much every day. The only time I'm not
here is holidays or Tết or if I'm sick; that's it.

I guess you could say it was my destiny to take up this
"profession" of selling chè. Yup, when I graduated from high
school, I had a little capital and some talent for cooking, so I
decided to open a chè stall to help the family out and put aside
a little money for the future. At first, I thought I'd just do it
for a little while, but now I've been running this shop for close
to ten years. The way I see it, the work is easy, and I don't need
to struggle just to make some profit. I take good care of my
customers and the chè I make is delicious, so it almost sells itself.
I make good money and I still have time to look after my little
family.

My day selling chè always comes with its happy moments.
People don't just come by for chè, but to meet friends, chat, share
stories, and of course exchange a little gossip. After one or two
visits, a lot of folks turn into regular customers; pretty soon they
stop by to say hello or to give me a little gift whenever they're in
the neighborhood. Just a little something, mind you, but I'm still
touched just knowing they were thinking of me. People here really
live with a lot of feeling, you know? Just about everyone in the
commune knows each other. And with selling chè here, I especially
get to know all the other ladies in the market; you get to be really
close working side by side every day, we treat each other like we're
all part of one big family.

This job also comes with its challenges though, mostly because the number of customers isn't steady; it all depends on the weather. In order to bring in more customers, I'm always learning to make all the new kinds of chè and finding new ways of making my chè even more appealing. I find a lot of joy in discovering new recipes and ways of making chè, because it's a way of sharing my love of cooking with my two little girls. Speaking of family, I've got two little ones, the youngest is in the seventh grade, and the oldest is in eleventh grade. They know I have to work hard, so they're always hardworking and gentle with their mom.

If you ask me, having a stable job like this and a cheerful, happy family is already everything I could ask for. I'm happy with my work, and up till now I've never even thought about changing jobs. Life in Bình Liêu is really simple and peaceful, and I just feel comfortable here; I don't have to struggle in the hustle and bustle like folks who live in the big city. So I take it easy and live one day at a time, why should I waste my time thinking and worrying? I'm content with my work and with my life; as for the future, whatever happens, happens. That's life, after all: nobody knows what the future will bring; we just have to do our best in the present, and let the future take care of itself.

Bình Liêu, July 2011
Hoàng Minh Trang

phở cook

My name's Quyến, and I'm 22 years old. I've been selling phở
for five years now. This is a traditional family business: my dad
started the restaurant, and now my brothers and I are helping him
run it. We're from Đồng Sơn village, in Nam Định. Nam Định
province is known as the birthplace of phở, so that's why so many
restaurants say they sell "Traditional Nam Định beef phở." Almost
the entire population of my village sells phở. You may come
across people selling phở from other villages, or even from other
provinces, but at least in Hanoi it's mainly people from Đồng Sơn.

When you're making phở, the most important thing is the
broth. Before we can sell a single bowl of phở, we have to cook the
broth for an entire day and night, so we have the fire burning and
the broth boiling 24 hours a day, seven days a week. The broth
you're eating right now had already been cooked for 24 hours
before we poured it into that big serving pot over there to continue
boiling. When a customer orders a bowl of phở, that's the broth we
use. We use that broth the whole day, and if there's any left over at
the end of the day, we dump it out.

Nam Định beef phở is not much different compared to other
phở. In the past, phở noodles from Nam Định had to be dried
by hand, but we don't have to do it that way anymore. Now,
people dry it by machine. The main difference is that it's part of a
tradition that's been passed down from one generation to the next.
Each phở shop has its own flavor; it's only when you eat it that you
can tell the difference.

Selling phở is a funny thing. Sometimes, we run out of phở in
the middle of the day; other times, there's still plenty left at the
end of the day. Even on a day when there's plenty of broth left over,
we throw it away; we have to. I know some phở shops put their
broth from the day before in the refrigerator to use again, but I can

guarantee that no Nam Định phở shop would ever do that.

Every day is the same: I work from dawn to dusk. My only time off is at Tết; that's when I go back to my hometown on the thirtieth and come back to work in Hanoi on the third day of the New Year. On other holidays, like Independence Day, I still have to work while other people get their day off. But I'm used to it. Once in a while, one of my friends asks me to hang out in the afternoon when we've got fewer customers; other times my brothers and I switch shifts for each other.

My family may work for the rest of our lives, but I can't imagine us ever buying our own house in Hanoi. My family didn't open a shop in our hometown because people in Nam Định don't have enough money to afford phở. So six years ago, my dad and my brother came to Hanoi, rented this house, and opened the shop. I came here one year after they did. I live in the shop. I'm the youngest; my oldest brother doesn't live here. So usually, it's only my other brother and me. Every day is the same, looking at the streets of Hanoi; it's the same. I guess it's because I'm used to it.

This shop is my dad's, I just help him. Business isn't growing much. To tell you the truth, life here is only a little better than life back home in the village. The price for one bowl of phở keeps going up because the price of everything else keeps going up. Six years ago, we rented this house for 6 million đồng [$300], and now the rent is 12 million [$600]. That's just in six years! And aside from rent, we also have to pay tax: 300,000 đồng [$150] each month. We don't make much profit; it's only enough to eat. And as for me, I don't actually get a monthly salary because I'm working for the family, you know? If I ever decide to do anything else later, I'll ask my family: if they have money they'll give it to me, if they don't, then I'll just have to accept it. I'm not sure what my future will be like, but if there's an opportunity, I might change my job. If not, then I guess at some point I'll have to break away from the family and open up my own phở shop.

Before this, I was studying in the village high school but I had trouble keeping up. And anyway, my family didn't have the resources for me to continue school, so I quit and came to Hanoi to sell phở. To tell you the truth, I want to become a car mechanic. Ever since I was a kid I've always played with cars, and back home in Đồng Sơn I would sometimes practice fixing cars. I don't really like selling phở, I like working on cars better. I told my parents about my dream several times but I know it's not easy.

Going to school and getting training cost money, and I'd have to ask my parents for it. And as you can see, we don't make much money selling phở, so I don't feel comfortable asking them for money. Sometimes at dinner my parents will say, "It's up to you, if you want, you should go to school," but I keep thinking about it and it just doesn't feel right. I don't have enough passion to pursue school. And if I do end up going to school, there won't be enough hands to help out in the shop, so we'll have to hire someone else. It's complicated.

Hanoi, September 2010
Mai Nguyen, Trương Minh Giang, Carol Nguyen, John Tran, Đỗ Thu Hương

taco truck cook

My name's Vân, and I'm in my 50s. I was born and raised in Thôn
Đông Lưu in Huế, Vietnam. My family and I came to the United
States in late 1995. Coming over to the States was a dream that
actually came true, but I couldn't linger on that dream forever. As
a matter of fact, I knew what I needed to do once my family settled
down: I needed a job! It wasn't just about keeping my family alive,
it was so I could build a brighter future for my children.

At the time, it was really popular for Vietnamese people to
become nail technicians. I must admit I was tempted to get a nail
technician license, but in the end I didn't do it. The next two
popular — or should I say available — jobs for Vietnamese people
who just migrated to the US were to work at phở restaurants or
food supermarkets, and that's exactly what I did. I applied to be a
chef at a phở restaurant.

Each shift was long and horrendous. Basically, I had to work
from 9 a.m. to 9 p.m., Monday to Sunday. Since I didn't know
any better then, I didn't complain about the long hours, not to
mention the terrible working conditions and the low pay. But
after a while I realized that I couldn't go on working like that, so
I ended up leaving the job. Soon enough, I was looking for my
second job. I applied to work at a nearby Vietnamese supermarket,
and I was fortunate enough — not having any experience or
English-language ability — to get accepted. Each shift was still
long and horrendous, but the working conditions were better. And
the pay was, well, still really low, but I knew that beggars can't be
choosers. Therefore, out of the two, I felt really fortunate to have
gotten the supermarket job.

I knew finding a job to make money was important if I wanted
to build a future for my kids. However, at the same time I felt

like I couldn't sacrifice 12 hours to work everyday, especially when those 12 hours were right in the middle of the day, making it almost impossible to see my family. After all, even though I'm working for their well-being, I still can't ignore the fact that they need to have a mother around to take care of them. Two years later, when my youngest started school, I realized that I had to find another job where I could see my kids when they came back from school. With the restaurant or supermarket jobs, I could only walk them to the bus stop every morning; I was never there to cook lunch for them or see them come home from school, not to mention the fact that we never had dinner together as a family. So in 1998, I quit my job at the supermarket — seeing my kids come home from school was more important to me.

Not long after I quit, a catering business approached me and introduced me to my current job. I don't cater at weddings or birthdays, instead I cook in a van and cater breakfast and lunch for construction workers. Yes, construction workers. And yes, the van is also known as a "taco truck." And before I knew it, catering became my career.

At 4 a.m., Monday to Friday, my alarm clock rings and I wake up and head to work. Work is very close to home, so by 4:30 a.m., I'm already there at my "second" kitchen. I prepare and cook for two hours straight, and then at 6:30 a.m., the driver, who's also my boss, and I get moving. Our destination is pretty far out of town, so we get there at 8 a.m., and then for the next four hours we drive from one construction site to another, selling breakfast and lunch. As for our own lunch break, the driver and I eat lunch whenever there's free time. I never had a set lunch time before so I don't mind. I can usually grab a bite or two while I'm cooking. We get back to town around 2 p.m., then we clean and restock for the next day. Then after a long day of work, I can finally go home and see my family.

This job usually needs only one cook and a driver. The relationship between the driver and me is usually very good. We're on the road most of the time, so we have a lot of time to talk, gossip, and just joke around. Then when we arrive at the work sites, we usually hold conversations with our customers. One of the things I like most about this job is that none of us, neither the customers nor I, know much English. But that doesn't stop us from trying to communicate. In the end, we usually end up just laughing with each other. In this job, there's always laughter!

The downside of this job is that it doesn't come with a vacation package. I get frustrated when I know my family has to cancel a vacation because I can't make it. On the upside, though, I usually get the important holidays, like Thanksgiving or Christmas off. My family tries to work around my schedule, so when we do go on trips, we go on the weekends when I'm not working.

Like everything, this job has its good and bad sides. But I can honestly say I believe I was born to cook. I really don't feel like there's any other job that would fit me better than this one.

Stockton, California, July 2011
Chieu-An Ton Nu

KFC employee

My name is Thủy, and I'm 18 years old. I'm from Việt Trì, but these days I'm living in Hanoi, going to high school full-time, and working part-time. Maybe you've seen me at the KFC on Nguyễn Trãi: that's where I work.

I chose to work at KFC because I'm able to communicate and connect with others while working here. I feel like KFC is my second family! It also gives me practical skills I can use in everyday life. It may not pay very well, but it's enough for me to live on, and they're flexible with my hours too. It doesn't clash with school. That's big. I also love KFC because before working there I worked at some clothes shops and they weren't so cool. I didn't have to work weekends, but my shifts were still 12 hours a day, from nine in the morning to nine at night. It's like the owners of the clothes shops, they may own the shop or a chain of shops, but do they have any sympathy for their employees? Well, obviously not when they know that we haven't had any lunch yet and they don't say a word. And when I finally do get to go for lunch at like 2 p.m. — yeah, 2 p.m.! [*laughs*] — they still yell at me, saying, "How on earth can you leave the shop and go for lunch?!" KFC's not like that. I've been working here for a long time now and my manager is way nicer than the people at the clothes shop. I mean, honestly, my salary is a lot lower here, but the attitudes of the managers and leaders are much better. They're so nice! And if they do yell at me, it's because they're trying to teach me to do things better. They know their employees and treat them like brothers and sisters, and there's no discrimination between managers and workers, or between new employees and those who've been there for awhile. We really are like brothers and sisters and we're always helping each other.

Before I worked here I didn't even know what KFC was [*laughs*]! A girl that was already working here introduced me, I sent in an application, and two weeks later I got an interview. Before, they would only use the "third-party recommendation" method for recruiting people. Like, I would have to work here for a few months and then I could help you get hired too. They didn't recruit people that somebody didn't already know. But now KFC

is having staffing problems, I guess because of the low pay or the hours, and now they have to hire externally. Actually, they hired a bunch of new employees for a new KFC but it hasn't opened yet so they're all still working at my restaurant — we have 40 people on staff in total, but officially only 35 work here.

So yeah, working here is good. I asked to work in the mornings during the week because I have classes in the afternoon. Then on the weekends I work evenings because I have classes in the morning. The managers are cool and work with my schedule requests so I do my best to stay in line and follow all the rules. My shifts are seven hours long, because eight hours would qualify as full-time. When I'm tired and the manager knows it, she only makes me work five or six hours. And since my house is far from work, she also lets me go home an hour early, so I get to leave at 10 p.m. when I work a night shift. I'm really lucky; it makes working here a lot nicer.

So yeah, I work on the lobby team. I do stuff like cleaning spilled food and refilling the chili sauce and ketchup. I think it's a good job for students: it's not physically demanding. There are a lot of different teams: lobby team, cashier team, supply team, cooking team, and managers. Each team has four or five members, depending on the team. The cashier team and the lobby team each have more members because there's more chance of advancement from there. The supply team usually has three members and the cooking team only has two.

Almost all the employees are women, except for those on the cooking team. Women are better at cooking, but cooking in KFC is totally different from cooking at home. It's really hot and strenuous; girls just can't take it for very long. Another reason is the cooking team only has experienced employees or people who are training to be managers. We call them "managing assistants" and they have to rotate through all the jobs in the restaurant before they can be promoted. The cashier team takes the money from customers, gives them change, and bags the food. Most importantly, though, they greet the customers. When you walk into a KFC you'll see the cashier team first, then the supply team behind them, and the cooking team in the back. If it's a small KFC, they'll put the cashiers on the first floor, supply team on the second, and cooking team on the third. It's the same in all the restaurants, just like the way the pay is the same too.

Since all the restaurants are connected and the employees can talk to each other, the salaries are set. If one KFC raises the salary, the others have to as well. It's a whole system and you can't have one manager deciding to raise an employee's salary, even if he knows they need it and sympathizes with them. Raises can only come from a higher manager: they're like 3000 đồng [15 cents] per hour for part-time workers and 300,000 đồng [$15] per month for full time.

For some people, a bad day at work is when they get yelled at by a manager or fight with a coworker. But I see things differently. Because I make mistakes and don't always do my job well, my manager or more experienced coworkers want to show me how to do things better. By thinking this way, I just treat conflict as a chance to learn from the experience. Others think, "Oh, the manager yelled at me. I quit!" Then they're never really going to develop a career. But I love working at KFC. I want to go to work every day to talk to my KFC family and friends. It's way better than sitting at home being bored!

Hanoi, October 2011
Sean Decker, Phạm Phương Thảo, Minh Thu Diep, Huỳnh Đình Quang Minh

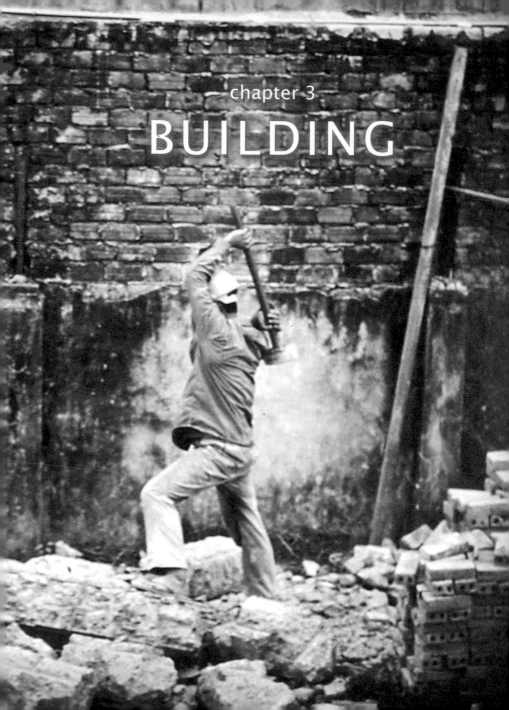

— chapter 3

BUILDING

construction worker

My name's Quang and I'm 42 years old. I grew up in Hưng Yên, and I've been doing this job for five years. My first job was working as a xe ôm [motorbike taxi] driver in Hanoi, but I changed to construction because there were too many xe ôm drivers by then. Nowadays, people have their own cars and use taxis more than motorbikes. And besides, with the streets so dirty, nobody wants to ride a motorbike if they don't have to.

We work in a team of five, and we're a lot like a family. I'm responsible for managing the team, but it's still like we're all relatives. All of us are from Hưng Yên, and each of us gets the same salary. No one is better or worse than anyone else, and I still get the same salary as everyone else, because at the end of the day we all have to do the same work. And even though I'm the leader, I still have to call some of my team members "uncle" because they're the younger brothers of my Mom or Dad [a reference to the family-based terms of address in Vietnamese].

In an average day, we work nine or ten hours. I start work at five in the morning and work through to noon. Then in the afternoon I work from two to as late as eight at night. On some days we only work until seven, but other days we have to work later. It's a hard job. We live on the job site, so we relocate often. The longest we ever stayed anywhere was half a month. Typically though, we stay at a work site for about ten days. Our clients don't provide us with room or board, so we use a tent. The members of my team and I have to care for ourselves and cook our own meals. Every day the team spends about 100 to 150,000 đồng [$5–$7.50] on expenses. And each person gets a salary of 100,000 đồng [$5]. So in a month, everyone gets about 3 million [$150]. If I lived in the countryside, 3 million would be enough for the whole family. But in Hanoi that kind of money just isn't enough.

Clients contact me by phone. We'll meet, discuss the work, and draw up a contract. After we finish building one house, the client's got my number and can recommend me to their friends. Clients these days ask for a lot of different things, but the more work we do, the more experience we have. And as clients get to know us, they start to see us as family.

Basically, this job isn't difficult. We have to know how to use the measuring equipment, and we need a certain amount of technical knowledge. If a client asks me a question, I have to know the answer. But that said, I've never had any formal training. I just learned on the job and through sharing experiences with the people I work with.

The main thing we have to focus on while we're working is avoiding having something heavy fall on us. We're supposed to wear protective equipment, but it's hot and uncomfortable. The government says we're supposed to buy insurance for ten years. But it costs 5 million đồng [$250] a year, and with the kind of money we're making, that's just too much. And me, I'm only doing this for a few more years, so it just doesn't make sense to buy insurance for ten years. If something happens, then the client will have to take responsibility for us. There's no other solution.

My wife stays at home and works on the farm. And my oldest son has already gone to work at a factory back in Hưng Yên. In one month he gets about 1 or 2 million [$50–$100], which is only enough to help his mom out. Before he graduated from high school, I encouraged him to study construction because some of our relatives were in the business. But he was sure he would pass the university entrance exam and he thought that learning a trade would just be a waste of money. When he didn't pass the exam, he decided to go work in the factory. My daughter is in the eighth grade now. If she wants to take the university entrance exam or go to college after high school, I'll try my hardest to support her education. I want her to study and become a kindergarten teacher because it's an easy job and it won't wear her down like other jobs.

I figure I'll keep at this for two more years. This job requires a lot of hard labor: if you're talking about construction work, it doesn't get any harder. People over the age of 40 really shouldn't do it. The lightest loads we carry are about 10 kilograms, and they can go as high as 450 kilograms. I still have the strength for this job for now, but I know it won't last forever. When the day comes, I'll go back to working in the fields with my wife. My kids will have their own families by then, and it'll just be me and my wife. If we need to, we'll find jobs that are light and easy.

Hanoi, September 2010
Mai Nguyen, Trương Minh Giang, Carol Nguyen, John Tran, Đỗ Thu Hương

surveyor

I'm Tuyến from Tiền Yên in Hoài Đức district and I'm a construct-ion surveyor. I joined the military in '81 and left in September '84. That December, the company I work for now visited my hometown to recruit new workers, so I applied. I started working for them on exactly January 1, 1985. In 1993, I moved my family to Hanoi to join me. My company is actually located right behind my house. I usually do the surveys for new roads and bridges. I go all over the North, and even throughout the rest of the country. I was once gone for four months straight before coming home. That was when I went to Sơn La. The farthest I've ever gone is Saigon. Basically, I just go wherever they need me.

If we work on-site then we don't get Saturdays or Sundays off. In the morning, we work from 7 to 11:30 a.m. We have a lunch break and then it's back to work from 1 until 6 p.m. If I'm not working on-site surveying, then I stay in my office to finish up project reports. I don't get paid if I'm not working. I can wait for work, but during that time, I won't earn a salary because it's based on how much work I do. They pay me a lump sum that includes earnings from reports and on-site work.

On-site work is harder than office work, so it pays a little more. I lead a team of ten people. I assign them tasks from 1st to 31st of each month — who does what on which day — and then I record it all in my construction log. I have to keep records of each project while we're working and even after the fieldwork is done.

Being team leader is a lot of work but that's why I get an extra 5 per cent of the earnings. When we're working on-site we normally receive 30 per cent in advance to cover our living expenses. When the project's finished, they give us another 50 per cent. The next 15 per cent is when we have an approved report. And the last 5 per cent we get for product warranty, after the project has been finished and has been in use for two years.

You can face a lot of problems from locals when you're working on-site. Some of them even threaten you with knives. It's happened more than once but you just have to be tough. You have to have a way with words, to talk them out of doing something to you. I remember one time when we were working in Thái Nguyên, these guys took out a big machete and tried to use it on me. As part of the surveying, we had to place stakes in their rice fields. I'd already notified the community but the residents didn't understand. When they saw me in their field, they started chasing after me and trying to hit me. I'd already put the stakes in the field. They ordered me to take them out but I refused. I told them that those were my orders and that they couldn't be reversed. That's it. They tried to fine me 100,000 đồng [$5] per stake but I still didn't take them out. I have to be tough like that; I just say it straight. Everything we do is legal; there's no need to take any crap from anyone.

We have to do surveys first before companies can design and construct new roads. It's a dangerous job. When you're working on the road, you're always afraid of getting hit by a car. Really, we've had casualties. Or a motorbike might hit you; that happens pretty often. About the worst that can happen is you end up with a broken arm or leg. Sometimes cars or motorbikes crash into the road meter, which was cheap to fix back in the day but nowadays costs 20 or 30 million [$1,000–$1,500]. The company will cover some of the cost — there's no way in hell we could cover it all — but usually we have to pay half of it. So if our contract says that the lump sum we're supposed to be paid is 100 million đồng, and the total cost of repairs is 20 million, we have to deduct 10 million from our end [$500]. The team splits whatever's left over, and it's actually pretty common to go into the red. In the end, the company may try to say that it's our fault because we didn't protect the meter carefully enough or for we didn't maintain it properly,

but it's never really our fault.

I do a lot of "outside work." Over the years, I've done projects for the government, for private companies, for limited liability companies and joint stock companies. I usually hire a team of five people, and I pay them by the day; nowadays it's about 400 or 500,000 [$20–$25] per day. Even if I have to pay them up front out of my own pocket, I do; I'll get reimbursed later. When you do that, you gain their loyalty. It's like the saying goes, "fresh money, real rice." When we've finished the project, it's my responsibility to get paid, and if I don't get paid, I have to deal with it. Sometimes, I end up losing money. For example, this one time I took on a 100 million đồng project [$5,000]. They paid me 30 million in advance, but when everything was finished, they wouldn't pay me the rest. In fact, they still haven't paid me.

These days, I'm a lot more careful. They have to pay me 50 per cent in advance, 30 per cent when the project's complete, and the remaining 20 per cent over the next three months. That's the only way I do it now. Secondly, there's gotta be a written contract — even if it's not legally binding — with the employer's personalized stamp and both our IDs as evidence. And last, it's gotta be precise: How much am I getting paid? When do you want it done? Give me a bullet point list of what you want me to do. That's all. I'll follow through with your bullet points, but if you want anything else done, then you're also paying me more. Only when everything's on the table, then I'll do it.

When anything needs to be measured, I'm the go-to guy; when it comes to surveying, I don't know the meaning of error. How much I get paid depends on how many kilometers I'm surveying and what type of road it is. If it's in a rural area, it's cheap. In the countryside, it's only about 10 million [$500] for a kilometer. But if it's a highway like Láng Hòa Lạc [which links Hanoi with new development areas to the southwest] then of course it's going to be expensive: 30 to 40 or even 50 million đồng [up to $2,500] per kilometer, for example.

In 2008, I did a 100 kilometer railroad project: it was just walking for 100 kilometers. The project took exactly two months and was located in Quảng Bình province. But it wasn't standard procedure: we had to walk back and forth, measure horizontally, vertically, every other way. We could only do about 20 kilometers at a time before needing to transfer over to the next train station, so it took five or six transfers before we finished the entire 100 kilometers. Since we were working for the railroad, they preferred us to stay at the stations or workers' homes; we were always warmly welcomed. Food was still at our own expense; they just provided the housing. And in return for the free housing, we treated them to drinks; hard to explain that expense in our records, but we found a way [*laughs*].

Last year, I took a trip to Singapore and Malaysia for the first time. I couldn't stop thinking about it when I came back: the infrastructure over there is just so different. The company sent us to check out the bridges and roads over there, just so we had an idea. But I can't even begin to imagine when we'll be able to build the kind of infrastructure they have over there ... [*sighs*] our country is still so poor.

Hanoi, October 2011
Nguyễn Thị Lan, Bùi Hà Phương, Tina Bao-Ngan Ngo, Annelisa Luong

tea company director

My name's Kỷ, and I'm Director of Kiên and Kiên Company.
The company specializes in exporting tea. In college I studied
Import and Export. Before I founded K&K, I worked at several
different jobs without a lot of success. So in 1997, I decided to
focus exclusively on the tea business. Exporting tea is difficult. The
quality standards are high and everything depends on the weather,
the soil quality, and how well you care for the trees. That said
though, thanks to all the experience I've had in the tea business
since 1984, work is pretty easy these days. And the way I see it, tea
is the perfect consumer product: it's something people have to use
daily. Even if there's a serious economic crisis, consumers might
cut back on the amount of tea they drink, but they will never stop
buying it completely. In addition, tea is something that can't be
reused, so it means there's always going to be demand for tea.

With a lot of hard work, I've been able to build four factories:
one in Thái Nguyên, two in Phú Thọ, and one more in An Khánh.
Each factory sources its tea from its own region, so the different
soil and weather means that each factory produces different
qualities and types of tea. Altogether, the four factories employ
about 300 workers, with annual production of around 8,000 to
10,000 tons of tea and turnover of about $10 million. Each factory
is financially independent, so my job entails working with the four
factory directors to plan, coordinate, and implement decisions.
Particularly from June to September, I'm on the road a lot. There
may be weeks when I spend every day at one of the factories
helping to motivate people. Or sometimes when we have problems
with supply and we don't have enough of the required ten
varieties of tea, I'll have to go to the factories myself to oversee the
production process until we're able to give our customers the right
types of tea at the right quality. But thanks to all our hard work,

today we supply anywhere from 5 to 10 per cent of the contents of every bag of Lipton tea.

In my view, the keys to success in business are commitment, intelligence, and customer service. Both acumen and determination are crucial if you're going to make the right decisions at the right time. At the same time, you can't overestimate the importance of creating and managing customer relations. Customer relations depend mainly on the director, and reflect the overall culture of the company. My secret for building customer relations is making sure that both sides benefit from the relationship; for example, I'll gain more from a contract this time, but you'll gain more the next time. With that kind of give and take, both our businesses can develop and prosper.

We specialize in export, so that means we've got customers all over the world. We have a presence in Chile, England, Russia, Germany, Holland, and more. New customers can either discover us through the Ministry of Trade, other customers, or our outreach efforts. I was once on a trip to Saudi Arabia with a commerce promotion group led by the Deputy Minister of Trade. I was so impressed; we stayed at a seven-star hotel where all the fixtures were inlaid with gold, and they invited us to go shopping at a mall where 90 per cent of the products were imported from Europe.

My job at K&K is my passion; it really inspires me. At the same time, it's also a way to help create work for other people, so that adds a lot of meaning to my life. I have to admit that the pressure of work can make life stressful sometimes. But that said, it's always the times when I've been under the most pressure that become my most unforgettable memories. The period when I decided to set up the four factories was the most difficult, complicated situation I ever faced; complicated because I had to look at the situation from so many different angles, difficult because I had to analyze every little detail, from the machinery to the factory building to the employees. But I'm satisfied with the results I've gotten from all my effort.

Everyone has their own ideas about how to live and be happy. As for me, I'm happy with what I have: enough money to live, a healthy and successful family, and a growing business.

Hanoi, November 2010
Lỗ Thị Lan Anh, Eliza Tran, Jennifer Phung, Nguyễn Minh Dương

chapter 4

MOVING

bus fee collector

My name is Hùng. I'm 31 years old and I work as a bus fee collector on Bus Number 39 for the Hanoi Bus Company. My work? It's just like any other job: it has its ups and downs. Every day is the same ... all I do is help the bus driver and sell bus tickets to passengers. I also check the passes of passengers who have monthly bus passes. And it's my responsibility to maintain order on the bus. Once I arrive at a point like a major bus station, I have to write down the numbers of tickets I've sold and give it to the employee at that station to check.

This profession is simple and straightforward, and it only lasts for a portion of the day. If I work in the morning, then I have to wake up really early because the first bus leaves at 5 a.m., but I get to go home in the afternoon. And if I work at night, then I don't have to begin working until the late afternoon. But I also have to check the bus after the last stop, so I don't usually get home until around 11 p.m.

If you want to know what it's like to work at a difficult job, then all you have to do is get on a bus during rush hour in Hanoi and ride it for a few stops. The volume of passengers on the bus is insane, so it's very difficult for me to check if everybody has a ticket. Moreover, most of the passengers are students, so no matter how crowded the bus gets, I still try to find a way to get them on the bus because I know how tiring it is to wait for another. However, this is also hard, because the more people I let on the bus, the more crowded it gets, which makes everybody hot and grumpy. Whether you work in the morning or in the afternoon, at least two hours of your shift are during the rush hour. In the winter, the crowd helps warm things up a bit, but in the summer, the heat is really too much. I guess this makes up for the times when there are barely any passengers [*smiles*].

But I've done this for a long time so I'm used to it. Crowds make me happy, and I also get a chance to chat with the students. It makes me feel younger and relaxed, and I forget how tired I am. That's one of the good things about this job. And anyway, I have no choice but to accept it. I'm used to it, and the job remains the same, so you have to find ways to make it more enjoyable, of course! That's how life is! There's no use complaining, it's best to be happy. Whether you're working at a temporary job or a permanent one, you have to remember to always love and value your work.

But if you want to work at this job, then you have to learn how to bear it as well as value it. You have to have strength, patience, and be willing to bear its difficulties, and be a little clever. You also have to have the energy to withstand the heat of a crowded bus filled with loud and agitated people. This job has really taught me to be more energetic [*laughs*]! And to think I've already stuck with it for almost a dozen years.

I don't make much money as a bus fee collector, but then

again, how do you ever know what's enough? You just have to try your best to save, in order to find ways to live and survive. In the beginning, my salary was really low, but it's increased significantly since then [*laughs*]. It's already more than enough to have a stable job. And with this job, I only have to work part of the day, so I can spend the rest of my time doing whatever else I want to do.

I'm currently going to school. I don't plan on staying in this line of work forever. But I'm not as lucky as other people. I wasn't able to pursue my education from the beginning. I didn't study much, so I had to first spend a lot of time trying to make a living before I could even think about going to school. My path to pursuing an education may be longer, but I have to study in order to find a more stable job. I also want to get married and have a family. But these days I make just enough to live; I don't make enough to live a decent life. So now, I go to work for part of the day, go to school for the rest of the day, and try to study on my own at home as well. It's the only way I can change my life and destiny. In order to live in today's society, you have to have knowledge. Studying is the only way to a better future.

Hanoi, September 2010
Tina Ngo, Nguyễn Hải Yến, Peter Del Moral, Đoàn Hồng Hải

railway crossing guard

My name's Kỳ, and I'm a railroad worker on the Hà-Hải line
[Hanoi to Hải Phòng]. I'm 50 now and I've been at this job for 20
years. I was originally an army man, but then I retired and built
railroads before switching to my current job. My main duties are
to close the barriers at the crossing when the train comes, and to
alert the train to stop in case there's a traffic jam or an accident at
the crossing. My group, which is responsible for the crossings from
Bạch Mai Hospital to Linh Đàm Lake, has more than 100 workers.
My team at this crossing has seven members in total; a normal
shift, which lasts 12 hours, requires two of us to be working at the
same time.

In general, we're responsible for everything when we're at the
crossing. If there's an accident, we're partially liable. Fortunately,
there aren't that many accidents. The government once tried
replacing us with an automatic barrier-closing system, but it failed
because people would always try to cross the tracks while the
barriers were closing, and there'd be traffic jams. Speaking of traffic
jams, it's much easier to work in the city where all we have to do
when there's a traffic jam is to call the train engineer on the phone.
When you're out in the countryside, you've got to go "catch" the
train and use lights and flags to get the engineer's attention ... it
can be quite dangerous. Sometimes the engineers stop at the wrong
place, which results in arguments ... then we have to write up a
report and submit it to our superiors.

The most tedious thing about this job is the way the trains
don't come on schedule: we only get about ten minutes notice
before the train arrives so we've got to stay at the crossing
for the whole shift. The day shifts are a bit better because 12
hours without any sleep can be really exhausting. It's also more

dangerous at night.

No one appreciates our work. We're just trying to keep people safe, but even so, people always complain when we close the barriers. We get insulted on a daily basis and sometimes fights even break out, but there's really nothing we can do about it. To do this kind of work, you've got to be gentle and know how to sweet talk; if you've got a bad temper, calling the police won't help even if you're right since it will take a long time for them to come and solve your problems. I once had an incident with some people but some locals intervened pretty quickly and nothing really happened. That was a long time ago [*smiles*].

Honestly, I don't find anything interesting about my job, but since I've been here for decades, I'm just trying to hang on and finish off my final years [*laughs*]. The railway industry's still state-owned so us workers are considered "state people," but we're so poor ... the highest our salaries go up to is a little over 2 million đồng [$100] a month. My family has a house here and both my two kids are grown up and in college now but we mainly live on the money my wife earns with her little shop at the market. What about people who have to rent a place to live? How are they supposed to live? My co-workers have also started selling prepaid mobile phone cards to earn a little extra cash. But if you're working outside the city, that's not an option. That's why the industry lacks workers ... we don't even want our children to work here. I've got about five years left before retirement and I haven't thought of anything to do after. I'm pretty sure that I wouldn't continue working here no matter how high a salary they offered me. The job can kill you any time [*laughs*]!

Hanoi, November 2011
Colleen Thuy-Tien Ngo, Josh Mayhew, Mai Lan, Mai Quang Huy

wounded veteran
moving service owner–operator

I fought against the Khmer Rouge in Cambodia. Thank God I was fortunate enough to suffer only minor wounds during my service! After the war, I went back to being a farmer in the countryside until eight years ago, when I decided to start a wounded veteran moving service because I needed a job that would let me earn more money. I made my application with the government and they let me purchase one of these three-wheeled vehicles at a price of 25 million đồng [$1,250]. It used to be the case that in order to have this job you had to be a wounded veteran. Don't tell anybody, but nowadays anyone can do this as long as they have the money to buy the vehicle and purchase the license.

The type of vehicle I use for work is very popular in Vietnam. Unlike normal motorbikes, it has three wheels instead of two. It also has a high-horsepower motor similar to those you find in large-displacement motorbikes. In the back, there are two parallel rows of seats surrounded by a metal frame, and then covered with a roof. It's big enough to fit six people or almost any goods you might want to move.

The price of my service is 20,000 đồng [$1] per kilometer, but it's negotiable. When a customer calls me, I come and pick them up. I'm usually asked to move furniture or bulky items a motorbike can't carry. These days I work from seven in the morning to six or seven at night, but sometimes I work till later if customers need me. On average, I have three or four customers a day, which is barely enough to survive. I work every day of the week and only take time off when I have to business to attend to at home. If I don't work, I'll starve.

I like the job best when I have a lot of customers, which means

I can make a lot of money! I have to say, though, that doing this work isn't easy. For example, driving this thing can be difficult because it has three wheels. When I'm carrying too much weight, the vehicle becomes unstable. Traffic is difficult to deal with as well, but everyone in Hanoi has to deal with that! Also, with the amount I'm driving, the vehicle needs constant maintenance; it's difficult and expensive to fix. Many shops don't even want to work on it. Repairs generally cost between 500,000 and 800,000 đồng [$25–$40]. Another problem is rising gas prices, which make it very difficult to make a profit. I also get completely soaked when it rains! There are so many challenges and difficulties that I can't even begin to explain them all to you. Honestly, I'm not particularly passionate about this job; I do it because I have to.

Memorable moments? It's hard to think of any in this job [*pauses, laughs*]. Actually, one time when I was making a delivery, there was a woman who was teasing me about getting married. She was about 36 years old and had been married before. Maybe she thought I was enthusiastic, handsome or just charming ... anyway, she actually suggested that I move over to her place! I didn't go for it because my conscience wouldn't allow it. Anyway, I only make enough to survive and support my family, so if I had a mistress there wouldn't be enough money to go around [*laughs*].

I currently live in the Trung Văn area of Đống Đa district in Hanoi, along with two to three other guys in the same line of work. I take care of myself, wash my own clothes, cook my own breakfast and dinner at home, and eat lunch on the street. My wife doesn't live in Hanoi with me. She lives in the countryside and works as a farmer. We're both Party members.

We have two kids. My son is a third-year university student and my daughter is in the eleventh grade. My boy studies at the Civil Engineering University. I don't live with him because it's not convenient. He lives much closer to his school, so he can benefit from daily interactions with the other students. He comes over to my place twice a month to visit me and get some money. I give him about 1.8 million [$90] per month, a little bit each time; if I don't I'm afraid he'll spend it all on his girlfriend. Actually, he's quite independent and thoughtful. He works part-time and was able to save up enough money to buy a motorbike last year. He'll get married soon, to his girlfriend who studies at the same school. But my daughter is still young; I don't want her to be in a relationship or fall in love too soon. She likes to talk back to us, but it's because she's really smart and does well at school. With luck, she'll be able to pass the entrance exam to attend the Hanoi National University of Education, in Cầu Giấy district. I've already bought a 40 square meter piece of land for her to build a house on and have a family. I'd like her to become a teacher even though she won't make a lot of money. Too much money can spoil a woman.

My family members worry about each other a lot, especially because of the way we have to live apart for financial reasons. Honestly, I'm more interested in working in my hometown, but this job provides for my family and their future. Working at home just won't bring in enough. If I were still young, I could make a lot of money driving my vehicle. Now, I'm already pushing 50, and it's getting a lot harder to make money. I also feel like this job is making me age even faster. At my age, I can't take the dust and pollution anymore. I'll probably do this for another year or two, then I'll go back to the countryside and become the head of the village cooperative. It's more suitable for me at this age, you know? People respect and listen to you more when you're older.

Well, it's dark now, let's drive home!

Hanoi, October 2011
Haven Rocha, Hoàng Huyền Trang, Ngoc-Diep Tang, Vũ Phương Thảo

motorbike parker

Ladies and gentlemen, I would like to take this opportunity to welcome you to my family's monthly motorbike parking service [*laughs*]. Allow me to introduce myself, I'm Vân, the chairperson of this "family economic cooperative" [*laughs*].

I was born and raised in Nam Định. In 1979, I graduated from high school. I was 18. Then, I went to Thái Nguyên to study to be a technical worker. After three years, I was assigned to work in "Tool and Equipment Factory #1," where I worked as a highly-qualified turner. Things were fine, but everything suddenly changed when I was diagnosed with ovarian cancer. Because I needed an operation, I was forced to change my job. So, in 1998, I became a cook in the factory cafeteria. I ended up working there until I was given early retirement in 2006. Since then, I've worked at all sorts of jobs. I was doing some odd jobs for Alfresco's [a Hong Kong-based chain of upmarket restaurants selling Western style food] for a couple of years before I gave myself a "second retirement" [*laughs*], and started to work full-time running this parking service out of our home.

Actually, my family's been working in the motorbike parking business since 1996, when we started looking after customers' motorbikes for the vendors at the market in Hanoi Mechanical Factory's collective area [which included the Tool and Equipment Factory #1]. After the market was closed in 2002, we changed the business model a bit. It's based in our home now, and since I'm retired, I've changed the availability of the service and pricing options to a 24-hour, pay-by-the-month model.

Honestly, though, I don't do this because I want to. The income isn't that great; I get 150,000 đồng [$7.50] a bike each month, and the most I can really make a month is 2 million đồng

[$100] because the space we've got can't hold more than 15 bikes. Also, the cost of living goes up every day, so even if I could change my fees to account for rising prices, inflation would still make it hard for me to match income with costs. Obviously 2 million đồng isn't enough to satisfy all of my family's needs.

Aside from not earning all that much money, motorbike parking is a poisonous and generally hazardous work for anyone. Clearly, breathing gas fumes all day can't be good for you, and gas is flammable so a fire breaking out is definitely a possibility too. And this is only one potential danger; there are a lot of other workplace hazards like being burned by hot exhaust pipes or getting crushed by a falling bike.

My job is more than just dangerous though, it's also exhausting. You have to be strong, both physically and mentally, to arrange the motorbikes so that you can bring them in and out quickly and efficiently. It gets particularly bad during rush hour, which happens twice a day, day in day out. During rush hour, I just get dizzy and worn-out. The pace of work is just so frenzied; I'm moving bikes around really fast while more and more people arrive to check bikes in or out. Still, the most difficult aspect of this job has to be our responsibility to our customers to remain open and available 24/7. Because of our 24/7 pledge, my family can't ever go out together. There's just no way we can leave the shop unattended.

Yeah, some neighbors have complained about the noise and the stench of gasoline during the night, but as time has passed, they've all learned to live with it. In fact, they can sympathize with us now, primarily because more and more first-floor families in our apartment building have decided to join the business themselves. Now they even try to compete with us [*laughs*]. But in all honesty, the level of competition isn't that serious. It's surprising maybe, but it is actually decreasing. Motorbike use is increasing quickly and so is the demand for parking space. In our neighborhood alone, for example, there are only four families who run parking services, and yet there are dozens of families and students living on the upper floors who need somewhere to park their bikes. So essentially, as long as we've got space, our customers are satisfied. Furthermore, our family's service is 100 per cent wholehearted.

No, I'm not concerned that we're ever going to run out of customers who need a place to park their bikes. But that doesn't mean I want to do this forever. I only want to do it until my kids are grown up and my family's situation improves because this job is dangerous and time-consuming. But for the time being, this is the work that helps me support this family, so, from the bottom of my heart, I'll live up to our pledge to provide customers with "friendly, careful, and conscientious service."

Hanoi, September 2011
Mai Lan, Mai Quang Huy, Colleen Thuy-Tien Ngo, Josh Mayhew

tourism company director

Chào anh, great to see you again! How are you doing? Beer? Is Saigon đỏ okay? Cigarette? Here, let me light that for you. So you want to hear about the career path that brought me to owning my own tour company? How long have you got, because over the years I've done more jobs than I can remember. And mind you, some of the ones I remember I really wish I could forget. But I guess all I can do is start at the beginning and finish at the end and see what sort of stories come out along the way.

I was born in 1968 in Gò Công, in the Mekong Delta, during the height of the war. Our village was in what they called a "free-fire zone," and the fighting was so bad that year that my mother didn't dare travel the few kilometers to the government office to register my birth, so all my paperwork says I was born in 1969. It was the same for all my buddies growing up; officially, I don't think there was a single child born in my village in 1968 [*laughs*].

I was the middle kid of a big family: me, my six brothers, and two sisters. Growing up in a village in the Mekong, you start work pretty young. Even before you go to school, you're doing simple things like shooing birds and chickens away from the paddy when it's spread out to dry in the yard. And it's not like the work stops when you get old enough to go to school, no way! Back then, we'd go to school in two shifts: if you went to school in the morning, you'd work in the afternoon and vice versa. Of course, you're not big enough to do the work of an adult, but you're still helping out, doing things like weeding the fields or handing the rice seedlings to the women as they're planting the fields. If you're really good at it you can take care of ten planters, but when you're little you're lucky just to keep up with three or four, walking along behind them in the mud, watching each of them like a hawk so as soon as they start to run out of seedlings, then whoop! you've handed them a fresh bunch so that they never have to stop for even a second.

When you're a kid, the work you do is just part of the general exchange of labor in the village. If I worked on the neighbors' field one day, then one of their kids would come over and work on our field another day. And with our family being as big as it was, we had a lot of labor to exchange, so we did pretty well [*laughs*]. We didn't use a clock or anything, we just followed the basic rhythm of the sun: there was the morning shift from about 5:30 or 6:00 to 10:00 a.m., and then the afternoon shift from about 2:00 to 6:00 or 6:30 p.m. When the sun is high in the middle of the day, it's just too hot to work. If school was out and we were working through the day, then after we were done working for the morning we'd make lunch and have a rest in the trồi [tent/temporary shelter built in the field]. For lunch, all we'd need to bring from home was some cooked rice and a little fish sauce. Back then there were so many fish, prawns, and crabs in the fields that it was easy to catch enough for lunch and then cook them up on some dried straw. So delicious!

I loved fishing and crabbing when I was a kid. Back then we only grew one crop of rice a year, so the fields were flooded for more than four months every year. You wouldn't believe how many fish, prawns, and crabs there were. When the tides were highest, all you had to do was open the sluice gates to let the water into the fields as the water rose. Then as the water started to recede, you'd put a trap in the sluice gate and from one field alone you could get ten kilograms of every kind of fish. So easy!

But my favorite was catching cua biển [mud crabs]. There're lots of different ways to go crabbing of course: you can use a rod, you can use a trap, you can even just feel around for them in the bottom of the flooded fields. Look, I've got the scars to prove it [laughs, shows scars on his hands and arms]. I don't know why, though, but I always found crabbing with a rod to be the most exciting. You'd prepare a bamboo rod and line with a little clay weight and some water snake meat for bait. You've got to use water snake for bait because the flesh is tough and it takes the crab longer to eat it. If you're experienced, you could prepare up to ten rods, spaced every 50 meters along one of the canals. And mind you, you'd have to stake out your canal early, or else all the best spots would be gone! So there you'd be, watching your rods and then pretty soon they'd start to bend with the weight of the crab at the bottom as he ate the bait. On a good day, you'd see all the rods bent over at once and you wouldn't know where to start first!

Then you'd have to run to the nearest one with your net, and try to bring the line up gently enough that the crab didn't notice, but fast enough so that he couldn't get away, like this: oop oop oop [*motions gently tugging the line up*]. And if you were lucky, then, whoop! you'd whisk him up in your net. On a good day with a nice high tide, I could get four or five kilograms of beautiful big crabs — really, claws on them like this! [*puts his two hands together to indicate the size*] — in just three or four hours. Incredible!

Of course, it's different now. I couldn't believe the change that had occurred in the years I was in the camps in Malaysia. By the time I came back to Gò Công in 1994, 80 per cent of the fish and crabs had disappeared. My little brother would come back from an entire day crabbing and all he'd have were three or four crabs barely bigger than your hand. What with the drive to increase the production of rice for export, the government built more canals to drain the land and make it possible to grow two or even three crops of rice per year. Well sure, that increased rice production at first, but it also disturbed the annual cycle of six months of fresh water flooding when the Mekong was high, and six months of brackish water from the influence of the Eastern Sea.

Basically, it destroyed an entire ecosystem. With no more brackish water, all the mangroves and water palms died. Without the freshwater flood, there was no silt to fertilize the fields so we had to buy synthetic fertilizers. And without the flood to wash away pests and insects, we had to use more and more pesticides. And after Vietnam opened up to the world after 1986 there were no more controls on the pesticides that were imported. We were using pesticides that had been banned for years in the West, like DDT, and every year we had to use more and more. I remember after we'd apply DDT to the fields, the smell from all the dead fish was disgusting. I don't know why, but most of the pesticides came from Switzerland. Great, isn't it? They ban it in their own country and then sell it to us. Today, the fish and the crabs are gone completely. We used to grow one crop of rice a year, but we were rich because of all the fish. Now we grow three crops of rice a year and yet we're driven into debt buying fertilizers and pesticides.

When I was 15 years old, I "turned professional." That means I was strong enough and experienced enough that I could hire myself out for wages rather than just taking part in the village's labor exchange. And you know, it's true. With all those years working in the fields, your knowledge becomes almost instinctive. Even today, after all these years living in the city, all I have to do is glance at the sky to know whether it's going to rain, or look at the moon to know whether it's a good time to go fishing.

I graduated high school when I was 18. My dad had been a private in the army of the Republic of Vietnam, so that meant my first job after graduation was my "labor duty." The male children of soldiers who fought for the Republic had a choice: they could perform one and a half years of "self supported" duty where they provided their own food, or three years of duty with food provided by the state. Well, of course I chose the first one. Mind you, in the end it wasn't just one and a half years, because your duty wasn't calculated in days, it was calculated in labor. Specifically, you had to work on canal projects, digging exactly six cubic meters of earth every day, five days a week, for 84 weeks. Have you ever had to dig six cubic meters of earth in a day? If the clay is dry and you're a strong young man like I was, okay, maybe you can do it. But what about when it's flood season and you have to dig exactly two meters deep into the flooded river delta? Or when it's raining? Or when you have to clear a forest and cut through the tangle of old roots? Even working in a team, there was no way to meet the daily quota. In the end, I was finally discharged after two years and three months. Somewhere at home I must still have the certificate I received from the government saying that I had "performed my duty" [laughs]. Today it's just a yellowed piece of paper, but it cost me more than I can ever say.

That period really was the darkest in my life. It was also when I started making the plans that led me to my next job. Back in 1985 I had to go to prison for a month for helping my older brother vượt biên [literally "cross the border," i.e., leave Vietnam illegally]. One of the older guys who was in prison with me kinda took me under his wing, and he decided to teach me a skill that, as he said, just might get me a free ride out of Vietnam some day. I don't know what his position had been when he'd been in the military; all I know is that he taught me how to navigate at sea with a map and a compass. So as soon as I got back home after my labor duty, I started putting my plan into action. Normally at that time, people in the country were paying two lượng [75 grams] of gold to get out of Vietnam; if they were rich Chinese in the city they were paying as much as ten lượng [375 grams]. Me, I didn't have any gold, but I did have a skill not many others did: I was an experienced navigator, of course! Eventually, I was introduced to a boat owner in Mỹ Tho. We met secretly one night, and you could see he was skeptical. Me, barely 21 years old, claiming to be an experienced navigator! It took me four hours to convince him, and it was only after he finally agreed at 2:00 a.m. that I learned why he was being so careful: it turned out his daughter would be on the boat with us. In the end, I managed to talk my way into a free passage for me and three of my buddies from the village; me as the navigator, two of my buddies because they had experience piloting boats, and one just because he was our friend [*laughs*].

If I look back at it now, it seems crazy. If we were lucky and made it to Malaysia, we'd face an uncertain future in refugee camps. If we were unlucky, we'd get caught by the Vietnamese Coast Guard and have to go to prison for two years. Even if we were lucky enough to make it out of Vietnamese waters, we'd still face the possibility of a breakdown at sea, hurricanes, or attacks by Thai pirates. I read a report once by the UN High Commission on Refugees where it said that of the 2.5 million Vietnamese who fled, one third of them never made it. I can't attest to that myself, but I can attest to the number of boats that I saw arrive in Malaysia with only one or two survivors on board. Those were the sorts of people who never really recovered from the experience: watching your child die of dehydration, watching your daughter get raped by pirates, being locked in the hold as they set your boat on fire, things that no amount of time can ever heal. Really, if I'd known then what I know now, I'd never have done it.

We left the Mỹ Tho pier at eight o'clock on a summer night in 1989. There were 27 of us on a little eight-meter fishing boat made for coastal waters. The oldest person on the boat was 42, and the youngest was 2. If everyone was on deck at once there was hardly room to move. There was no bridge to speak of, only four bamboo poles at the stern with some canvas strung over them to keep the sun off whoever was piloting the boat. Two days into the journey, we were out of Vietnamese waters and far into the Gulf of Thailand when we realized that there was a problem with the clutch. The engine was running fine, but the propeller simply wasn't spinning. My buddy put his head into the water and he could literally count the revolutions of the propeller, one, two, three... there were two guys on the boat who'd gotten free rides by claiming to be mechanics, but it turned out they knew even less about engines than the rest of us. One of my friends got so angry we had to hold him back or else he would have thrown both of them into the sea.

So there we were, just floating in the middle of the Gulf of Thailand as the weather closed in, and no one wants to call for help in case pirates spot us. The fourth night out was the worst; when the storm hit, the seas were incredibly high and without the propeller working there was no way to turn the boat into the wind so we could ride out the waves. We'd put the rest of the passengers in the hold while my friends and I tied ourselves to the deck and did what little we could to keep the boat from capsizing as these giant waves crashed over the side again and again and again. I still don't know how we made it through that night, but we did. The next afternoon, we made a decision: we'd just have to risk it and put up the international distress signal: three white boards nailed to a pole like this [*demonstrates with a combination of cell phones and cigarette cartons*], with my friend's white shirt flying at the top to attract attention. That's another useful thing I learned in prison [*laughs*]!

You have no idea how tense we were when the next day a boat saw our signal and pulled alongside. I looked up at the young Thai sailors staring down at us from the deck of this enormous fishing boat and I really didn't know if we were saved or if our ordeal was just beginning. But the captain of the boat was a good man. Within 20 minutes we were eating our first hot meal since leaving Vietnam. Me, though, I was too busy acting like a crazy man as I tried to mime a broken clutch. Ever had to do that? It's not easy [*laughs*]! But after half an hour of miscommunication, the ship's engineer and I were down in the dark of the hold, sweating like pigs as we tried to figure out what was wrong. After we got the clutch fixed, I wolfed down a bowl of rice then went up to the bridge with the captain where he plotted our course to Malaysia for us. Then they filled our fuel tanks, replenished our fresh water and we were on our way. They'd saved our lives and all we could do to thank them was to smile and wave as they pulled away.

Five days later, we finally reached an island off the Malaysian coast. The next morning they let us land and herded us into trucks under the guard of heavily armed soldiers. When I arrived in the camp, all I had were the clothes on my back and a piece of paper with my brother's address in Canada. You have to understand the context here: when the Soviet Union collapsed, the main receiving countries for Vietnamese boat people — the US, Canada, Australia, and France — met and decided that after March 14, 1989, we were no longer "refugees" but rather "displaced persons." From then on, instead of being granted refugee status in the West, we'd be "encouraged" to return to Vietnam. We'd arrived at the end of June — three months too late. Can you imagine? We'd risked our lives like this only to be sent back to Vietnam? Mind you, my friends and I weren't going to give up so easily. We decided to refuse the offers of repatriation and resist to the end.

So for the next four years, my life was lived out within the confines of a refugee camp. At times the boredom and the depression were almost too much to take. My one occupation was singing in the choir, if you can believe that. One of my best friends in the camp was a Protestant pastor, and when he noticed I had a good voice he recruited me for his choir. As Tết approached, we'd perform for people in return for donations of food. All the other groups had choirs too: the Catholics and even the Buddhists. By the time Tết arrived, my throat would be raw from all the singing, but it was all worth it, as much for the sense of community and sharing as for the extra food we got. But I have to say, the extra food was nice [*laughs*]!

Mainly, though, my friends and I spent our days nursing a coffee and telling stories at the little café one of the guards had set up under a tree in the camp. The ritual at the end of the day was always the same: one of us would head off through the camp trying to scrounge a few ringgit to pay the bill while the rest remained behind. Inevitably, the first one would came back and shake his head sadly, then it was time for the second one to try, and so on and so on. Somehow, though, one of us always found a way to pay. But after a while, my friend the pastor decided we should learn a skill in case we eventually had to go back to Vietnam. We'd been hearing that as the country opened up to the world, more and more tourists were visiting and creating a demand for English-speaking tour guides. And as luck would have it, the pastor had been an English teacher before 1975. So from that day onwards, instead of just swapping the same tired stories, we'd spend the day learning English with the pastor. Three, four, sometimes six hours a day we'd study, with nothing more than a pen, a notebook and an English-language Malaysian newspaper. I'll always remember when we got our first dictionary. My brother used to send me $50 every month, so as the wealthiest student it fell to me to buy it. I managed to get a Longman English Dictionary for 22 ringgit from one of the guards. Even though it was published on that cheap grey paper, to us it was the most precious thing in the world. For months after we got that dictionary, we were literally intoxicated with the words we found there.

We spent more than two years in that camp on the island, and then another two years in a much bigger camp outside of Kuala Lumpur before we gave in and agreed to be repatriated in 1993. I spent one season helping my family with the farm, but I just couldn't readjust to life in the countryside. At first I applied to be a guide with the state tourism company in Mỹ Tho, but with my background my application was never going to go anywhere. So in early 1994 I left to try my luck in Saigon. It was tough. I didn't have any family or friends in the city, and no one wanted to rent a room to a stranger from the countryside. I ended up taking a course in Microsoft Office at a vocational college just because the program included room and board. One day about three weeks into the course, my classmate and I had gone to the college, supposedly to prepare for the upcoming exam but mainly to take advantage of the air conditioning in the computer room. We were chatting with one of the teaching assistants when he happened to mention

that one of the tourism companies was looking for guides who had at least "B" Level English. In those days, the government had three levels of English language certification: A, B, and C. Now I'd never taken any test, but I knew that with all those years in the camp studying every day, my English ability was already well beyond any of the government's classifications. So my buddy and I spent the next three hours plying the guy with glasses of soy milk at the shop by the college gate until we finally got him to introduce me to his friend, who then introduced me to another friend who worked at the tourism company who introduced me to his manager.

When I finally got to meet him, the first thing the manager asked was whether I had my "B" Level certificate. I said no, but all he had to do was give me a chance and I'd get whatever sort of certification he wanted. I guess he had faith in me, because I started the next day. At first, my job was to hand out claim tickets to clients who wanted to leave their baggage with us while they went on tours. On the fourth day, there was space on a tour going to Củ Chi and Tây Ninh, so the manager told me to go along just to observe how it was done. The next morning I was handing out claim tickets as usual when I hear my manager screaming like he wants to tear someone's head off. It turns out one of the staff had booked a tour for seven people the night before but forgotten to enter it into the system. So there were no guides, no van, nothing except seven frustrated backpackers. After my manager finally calmed down, he gets on the phone and manages to borrow an old van from somewhere. Then he looks around the room at all of us employees, sees me, and says: "You, you've been to Củ Chi, right?" Minutes later I was collecting my salary — 4 USD, paid in advance — and preparing to lead my first tour. I'd made it: I was a professional tour guide.

I worked there guiding backpackers for three years, and then moved on to a company that specialized in upmarket tours. That's where I ended up meeting a couple from Melbourne who took a liking to me. They tried to arrange for a visa for me to visit Australia, but back then it was still really difficult for Vietnamese to go overseas. They didn't give up though, and they ended up introducing me to this lovely old Catholic nun who'd been working with Vietnamese refugees in the camps for years. I don't know what sort of connections she had, but one week after she'd met me at a café in Saigon, I was in at the Australian consulate picking up my three-month visa.

I arrived in Melbourne in the middle of their winter: I almost froze to death! But still I wanted to stay, so I decided to take advantage of a policy that allowed people to extend their visa if they were going to school, and I enrolled in a translation course at the local university The only way I could afford the fees was to work four shifts every weekend as a cleaner. The course was supposed to last two years, but all that time spent studying English under the tree in the camp was good preparation and they let me graduate in 2001 after just one year. A few months later I was earning my first wages as a government-certified interpreter.

The work was interesting and challenging, but as time went on I realized it wasn't the right job for me. The truth is, interpreters usually get called in when something goes wrong: for every one wedding you interpret for, there's a hundred divorces, arrests, and court cases. I remember one time I was called in for the interrogation of a big-time drug dealer: I couldn't believe my eyes as I walked through this maximum-security prison and saw they had air conditioning, TVs, a library, a gym, volleyball and basketball courts, the works! It was a little different from prison in Vietnam, let me tell you [*laughs*]. After a while I started to worry that if I spent all my time dealing with the worst sides of the Vietnamese community in Australia, my attitude toward my own people would start to change, that maybe I'd start to feel ashamed to be Vietnamese. So even when I was granted Permanent Resident status in 2003, I knew I could never stay in Australia. First, I knew I was doing the wrong job. But more importantly, those years working as a tour guide had really opened my eyes to the beauty of my country and my people. I guess you could say I was in love with Vietnam. So just six months after I got my Australian PR, I'd packed my bags and was on a plane back to Vietnam.

Within two weeks of arriving back in Saigon, I was working as a tour guide again. By 2004 I'd been appointed a manager for one of the big high-end tour operators, supervising a team of almost a hundred guides. It was a lovely job, really — the company director literally let me write my own job description. I chose to focus on quality control: choosing, training, and motivating our people to create the best team of guides in the country. I'd probably still be there if it weren't for the birth of my baby girl in 2007. When she was born, I realized that I really needed something of my own, something to pass along to my child; I couldn't just keep on working for other people forever. So that's when I started planning to start my own tour company. Step by step, I laid the groundwork until we finally took our first tour in the summer of 2010.

My company focuses exclusively on small, personalized, high-end tours that introduce our clients to the real Vietnam, instead of just shuttling customers from one tourist trap to the other. You know, I've been around the world, seen Asia, Australia, Europe, and America, and I still haven't found any place that can compare to Vietnam. I don't know how to explain it, but there's just something so wonderful about this country, the diversity from North to South and East to West, the cheerful people, the great food; man, I love it! It may sound corny, but my goal is for our customers to love this country like I do. Tomorrow afternoon I'm going to the airport to pick up the same Australian couple that was on my company's very first tour back in the summer of 2010. This will be their fifth tour with us, and they've recommended more than 50 other clients to us. To thank them for their support, I've organized a honeymoon in Vietnam for their son and his bride, all expenses paid [*laughs*]. Doing business this way is never going to make me rich, but it does allow me to share my passion for this wonderful place. Sure, life in Vietnam hasn't always been easy. Sure, living and working in Vietnam today has its frustrations. But for me, I just want to put politics and history aside and focus on sharing my love for Vietnam and its people.

Saigon, December 2012
Gerard Sasges

chapter 5

MAKING

statue craftsman

My name is Trần Khương and I'm from Xuân Bắc Commune in
Nam Định Province. Carving is a tradition in my family. When I
was a child, I'd often watch my father while he was working. Little
by little, I just taught myself how to make things out of wood.
In all, it's a tradition that has spanned five generations: from my
great-grandfather to my grandfather, from my grandfather to my
father, and now from me to my son. We're the only family in the
province who does this. Ever since the time of my father, Phó Gia,
our reputation has really spread, such that now our name is famous
not just in Nam Định, but throughout all of Northern Vietnam.
We've even had foreigners who've heard about us and came to
place an order.

   We're Catholic, so most of our work is statues of Jesus, the
Virgin Mary, saints, and other figures for churches. I do make
the odd children's toy sometimes, but just a few. If you compare
Buddhist and Catholic statues, I'd say the Catholic statues take

a lot more work: you've got to spend time on the smallest detail, from the facial expression to the fingernails. Take the baby Jesus, for example: the contours of his hands have to capture his chubby cuteness; with the Virgin Mary, the folds in her dress should make you feel the wind blowing. That's why I do most of my work at night: that's the only time I've got the peace and quiet I need to concentrate and really let my imagination take flight.

The carving process starts when a representative of a church comes to place an order. We'll discuss the exact dimensions of the statue, look at pictures to use as a model, and finalize any other details. Then we sign a contract.

Sometimes a customer will already have the wood they want to use, but usually they trust me to source the wood that best suits their type of statue. Generally, I use vàng tâm [*Magnolia fordiana*] and giổi [*Michelia hypolampra*] because they're very smooth, beautiful and durable, but still lightweight. Wood can't be used immediately: you've got to season it first or else it's harder to carve and the statue will deteriorate faster. Once the wood is properly seasoned, we cut it into smaller pieces so we can begin carving.

I carve by hand. After doing this job for so many years, I don't need to look at pictures to use as models anymore. I just listen to the customer's description and then use my imagination to turn their ideas into reality. I work on the individual parts of the statue separately. Once I've finished all the parts, my son or I will join them together to make the statue.

Next comes the painting. The paints they sell in Vietnam don't have the adherence and color-fastness I need, so I usually order my pigments from Japan or Germany. I mix the colors myself and filter them with cloth to get the exact shade I want. After each coat of paint, you have to let the statue rest until it's completely dry. Then you sandpaper it and add the next coat of paint. It takes five or six coats before it's ready.

Altogether, it takes more than a month for me to finish a one meter tall statue. Statues in Vietnam are much cheaper than in the West. One of my brothers lives in America now; he recently sold a two-meter tall statue for nearly $5,000, whereas I can only charge about $500 for the same statue. I still remember one time when an official from the Department of Culture visited our shop and exclaimed: "Oh my God, how can a beautiful work of art like this be so cheap?"

This job was much more difficult in the past. During the war and the subsidy period, the economy was tightly controlled and religious freedom was strictly limited, so an occupation like mine was prohibited. Instead, everyone in the household was required to work on the collective farm. The authorities confiscated my materials, tools, and statues. But working as a farmer on the collective couldn't provide enough to raise seven kids, so after a while I left and logged timber in the forests.

After the Đổi Mới reforms, controls on religions were relaxed. As churches reopened, they needed to be restored and repaired. But people were still very poor and didn't have money to donate, so I ended up offering most of the statues I made back then to the churches. Let's just say that a lot of statues were carved, but not much money was earned [laughs]. These days, though, things are a lot easier. People have money to donate to the churches, wood is widely available, and it's much easier to import my paints from abroad. I'm finally able to make a living doing the thing I've always loved.

I've always carved my statues myself. I only let my sons do things like painting or gluing. People ask why I don't make it easier on myself and hire someone. To tell you the truth, I did try hiring someone once. But the salary he asked for was high and his work didn't meet my expectations, so in the end, I decided to continue doing everything myself.

This is a really difficult job. Not everyone can do it. Very few people have the enthusiasm, patience, and commitment, combined with an aptitude for working with wood. I've never forced my children to follow in my footsteps, nor have I ever tried to run training courses for others. Fortunately, one of my sons has become a successful carver in his own right. Now he's the one who gets all the orders. It's lucky, because I'm old now and I suffer from terrible back pain; having my son here means I can concentrate on smaller orders and give my back a break.

This profession has defined me. It's part of a family tradition that links five generations together; how can I not love it? You can find the Phó Gia name anywhere there are wooden statues, from the smallest local church to the Phát Diệm Cathedral. No words can describe the pride I have for my profession. My only hope is that our family will continue to follow the tradition for generations and generations to come.

Xuân Bắc, November 2010
Nguyễn Minh Dương, Lỗ Thị Lan Anh, Eliza Tran, Jennifer Phung

áo dài tailor

After the war ended, my family was very poor. Most of us were, back in those days. That's why out of all us kids, my parents were only able to send my brother, the eldest and only son, to university. The rest of us stayed home and helped my mom make áo dài [literally "long shirt," the distinctive Vietnamese dress for women]. So that was it, five of us girls, with my mother and sister-in-law doing the training. My sister-in-law was a particularly big influence on my tailoring. She was a very talented tailor and a good teacher too.

So that's when I started making áo dài. It was 17 years ago, right after I finished high school. I'm 35 now and I still live and work in the shop where I learned to make áo dài. Originally, my sister-in-law owned the shop, but then she moved and my other sisters also got married or got different jobs so I was left with the shop. Sometimes, though, my sisters will still come and help out at the shop. That's always nice.

Being self-employed definitely has its benefits. I can work at my own pace and take breaks when I want. If I feel like leaving the shop for while, I'm free to do so. If I were employed by someone else, I'd lose a lot of my freedom and I'd earn a lot less too, because the boss would only give me a small percentage of the profit. I also don't have to pay any rent because the shop is in my house.

During the busy season, I can make 6 million đồng [$300] a month or more, sometimes even 7 or 8 million [$350–$400]. That's the absolute most I can make though, because I don't have any employees to help me. During the slow season, I usually make 2 or 3 million [$100–$150] a month. The fall is the busiest because a lot of students and teachers want new áo dài for the new school year. After that, it stays busy through Tết because that's the period when most weddings take place. Also, many people want new áo dài for the holidays. After Tết, my business slows down a lot. Most of my customers are high school students, teachers, bank tellers, flight attendants, and brides preparing for their weddings. I even have customers who are TV anchors.

The process of making an áo dài begins when people bring me fabrics. Then, I take their measurements. They tell me their preferences: long or short, tight or loose, collarless or with collar, what shape they want for the collar or the neck, how long or how wide they want the sleeves or the trouser legs to be, etc. Lastly, we make an appointment for them to come back to try it on.

I start by cutting the fabric; I use tailor's chalk to draw on the fabric and then cut along the line. Then I sew the pieces together, leaving the seams a little loose so I can fix it if the customer wants to tighten or loosen the áo dài anywhere. Then the customer comes for their first fitting. If they're pleased with everything then I secure the seams and make any finishing touches. If they want any changes, then I adjust the áo dài and arrange an appointment for another fitting. Usually, though, customers only need one fitting.

In total, making an áo dài takes me about two to three hours. I do every part of the tailoring process myself, except for the part called "luông." Luông is the process of making tiny, invisible stitches by hand at certain key places like the neck, the hemline, the front and back panels, and the places where you attach buttons. Because it's so time-consuming, I pay other seamstresses to luông; I can cut and sew several dresses in the time it takes to luông one dress. However, before I can send it out to the seamstress to luông, I first have to "lược" the áo dài. That's when I use a pair of small scissors to cut the threads of the rest of the stitches. That way, when you look at the áo dài, you don't see any stitches at all.

I usually charge 200,000 đồng [$10] for one áo dài: 150,000 for the top and 50,000 for the pants. Sometimes I'll charge a little more if the fabrics are hard to work with. Customers are generally very nice. The only time they ever get upset is if I can't finish their áo dài on time. But mainly, customers like coming to me because the áo dài I make are beautiful and nicely tailored to their bodies. Thanks to my sister-in-law, my tailoring skills are really top-notch. Other shops can't make an áo dài as beautiful as mine, or if they can, they charge much higher prices. That's why customers like coming to me.

As you can see, I've got a pretty stable career. No matter what

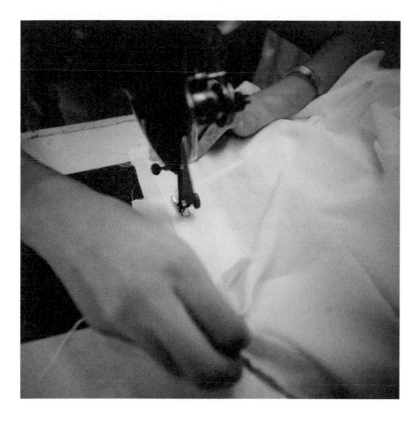

happens, there's always going to be a demand for áo dài. That's not to say this job doesn't have any challenges. Sometimes a customer wants their áo dài quickly, which puts me under a lot of pressure to get it done in time. Being self-employed means I don't have any insurance or pension. But I have to say, the worst part of the job is the chronic shoulder and back pain from sitting and sewing all day.

If I weren't a tailor, I don't know what I'd be. I don't have the skills for any other occupations, and I didn't go to university so I never had any other career options. Besides, why would I want to do something different? Tailoring an áo dài is an art; it's a lot harder than your average dress and or shirt. You've got to have a great deal of skill and pay the utmost attention. When someone puts on an áo dài, it has to fit perfectly from top to bottom; people can see immediately any mistake you made during the tailoring process. With other dresses, it's easier to overlook the mistakes; it's no big deal if you wear a dress that's a little loose on the top or a little tight on the bottom, you can still wear it. Not with an áo dài you can't. I guess that's what makes an áo dài so special.

Hanoi, November 2011
Nguyễn Thùy Trang, Lena Tran, Maya Weir, Vũ Thu Hiền

garment factory worker

My name is Kháng, I'm 31 years old. My hometown is in Hưng Yên and I've worked here in Sewing Factory Number 10 for almost ten years now. I decided to come and work at Number 10 because I knew a guy who worked here, and he told me to join him because the conditions here were really good. People in my hometown have been farmers for generations, so this is not really traditional work. But even so, my family didn't oppose me working here; in fact, they supported my decision.

I remember when I first got here, I had to study at the Number 10 training college for four months. When it was over, I had to take a test before I was hired. At first, I worked in the ironing section because they didn't have enough people. But after six or seven days, I switched over to the sewing section and I've been here ever since.

In 2005, I got married. My wife works here too. We have one little girl: she's in kindergarten now. The company has a hostel for workers to stay in where the rent is much cheaper than outside, but now that I've got my own family, I can't live there anymore. Luckily, we rent a house near the factory so it's really easy to go home when we need to. A typical work day for me starts at 7 a.m. and ends at 5:15 p.m., the lunch break is from 11 a.m. to 12:30 p.m. That's still enough time to make it home to cook for my wife and kid; the key is to cook the rice before I go to work [*laughs*]. And in the evening, my wife and I take turns; one of us does the cooking while the other goes and picks up our girl.

We're not in the same group at work though. I make the "three-leaf" shirt collars while she sews them: they're two separate tasks. Just making one shirt has, like, 20 separate steps: making the collars, sewing them, fitting them into the shirt, sewing the sleeves, putting the buttons on, and so on. Each person just

111

handles one task though, so it's pretty quick, you just get used to the task, you know [*laughs*]. The output varies, but typically, I can make around 1000 collars in a day. And I get paid by the piece, so it's easy to calculate your wage. It could be 5 million [$250] this month, or just 4 million [$200] the next, it depends. Altogether, my wife and I make around 7 or 8 million [$350–$400] a month; rent and utilities cost like 1 million [$50], so it's enough for us to live on.

About three quarters of the people who work here are women, but gender doesn't really matter. Whether you're a woman or a man, you just try to do a good job and not be dependent on others. It's not really the case that the job here is more suitable for women, you just need to learn the skills and you're good to go. We work in groups here. My group has around 10 people, and we've been working together for quite a while so we know each other well. If I have to move to another group, it's fine, but it'll take a while for me to get to know new people. My relationship with the other members of my group is good, you know, friendly and open. We all live around here too, so we hang out every now and then.

Every three to five years, employees can take a test to advance a level. There are five different levels, and now I'm at level 3. There's a chance for you to be a group leader, you know, if the bosses notice that you're doing a good job. When you're a group leader, your salary is calculated differently and your job is to supervise, not to sew. And employees can buy company shares too. The amount depends on the number of years you've worked — the longer you work here the more shares you're allowed to buy — but it's not compulsory. I just bought some myself [*laughs*].

The working conditions are pretty good: we've got insurance, holidays, vacations, sick leave, all that stuff. The company also organizes contests, performances, singing and other activities. Oh, and the company holds festivals for the workers' children as well, like at the Mid-autumn Festival [Tết Trung Thu, a festival particularly associated with children]. The company even arranges holidays for workers. We just go, and it doesn't even need to be an official vacation [*laughs*]. On occasions like that, the workers can bond and get to know each other better.

The working environment here is fine too, though there are some people who complain that the air is bad, with fibers and other stuff in it. The air is a little stuffy too, but we've got fans and air conditioning, so it's not as bad as it could be. And it's noisy, but it's a factory you know, what do you expect? I've gotten used to the noise so it doesn't bother me anymore. And on the bright side, it's always clean in here.

I've had tough times and met some obstacles on the job, actually. Like when I was starting off with the job or when we're making a new model. Then, you're not used to the work yet, and that's when you have problems with quality. But after a while you get used to it and everything's cool [*laughs*]. And work here is pretty stressful, you've got your quota, and if you don't meet it then ... [*trails off*]. The company demands a certain output depending on the model and the season, but typically it's more than a thousand a day. For the new models, they might lower the quota 50 or 70 pieces; it depends. Each group has their quota. One group can be more than 1,000 while other groups could be more or less. It depends on the particular model. And then whichever group has the fewest workers but the highest output gets the red flag. The group with the lowest productivity gets the yellow one [a reference to actual flags that hang over the workspace of the groups with the highest and lowest productivity].

There are many good memories that come with the job, but the best was probably when I got married [*laughs*]. All our relatives and the workers in the factory came to wish us a happy marriage. It was a lot of fun. After almost 10 years on the job,

I've learned a lot, become more mature, and made some good friendships. Still, it's hard to say that I'm satisfied. No matter what you have, you always want more, you know? But to tell you the truth, I don't really know what I would do if I didn't work here. I just try my best to do a good job and if something changes in the future, we'll just have to see how it goes. I've got a family now, so whatever decision I make, I have to consider things carefully. In the end, what motivates me to work is taking care of my wife and kid and supporting the family.

Gia Lâm, October 2011
Tracy Nguyen, Trương Công Tuấn, Đinh Đoàn Vũ, Nguyễn Thanh Nga

electronics factory worker

My name is Tiến. In Saigon, I had a small shop selling spices and cooking supplies at Gò Vấp Market. I sold it when my family emigrated to the US. That was almost 5 years ago. Now, I work at a factory on the prepping line in Houston, Texas. Before this, I worked as a babysitter for about a year.

Working as a babysitter was a good job. Sometimes I helped with cooking and cleaning, but my primary task was taking care of one-year-old Hannah. I played with her, taught her how to walk, and sang her lullabies as if she were my own daughter. I made about $1,000 a month babysitting; it's about the same amount I get at my current job. As a babysitter, I stayed with the family I worked with on weekdays and went home on weekends. I felt bad that my husband was by himself for most of the time because our three sons still live in Vietnam.

Now, I work in an electronics manufacturing company. In the morning, I go to work with my husband. He works in the soldering line; I work in the prepping line. It usually takes us about 10 to 15 minutes to get to work, depending on the traffic. I clock in at 7 a.m. and clock out at around 3:45 p.m. My job is hourly-waged. My shift is eight hours long, and we get two 15-minute breaks and one 45-minute unpaid lunch break. My job doesn't require many skills or much experience. Just about anyone can work here.

My group, made of four people, just follows the models and instructions they give us. If the models are complicated, we have to be more attentive. My job is preparing the materials so the next group in the assembly line can solder them. We split the work, and each one of us masters a different task to reduce mistakes. The job is very simple and not very challenging at all. The only training necessary for this job is watching and learning from the people who've been working here longer — they're really nice and helpful. During break times, they show us newbies tips and strategies to get work done.

When I'm not working, I walk around the factory for some fresh air and exercise. Other times, I sit and chat with my co-workers over some biscuits and hot tea. We just talk about our work experiences and share our skills and techniques. These conversations are always interesting to me, especially because I can learn English from them. My English has improved a lot from interacting with my co-workers every day. There are words that I would never remember unless I heard someone say it or if they explain it to me. That's one of my favorite things about this job.

There are also many good things about my job. I get a lot of benefits: vacation time, health insurance, sick days, and all that stuff. The only thing I would want to change is my salary; it's not as high as other companies'. However, I'm in no position to complain. In this economy, I'm lucky to have a good job with a lot of benefits. It scares me that I can be let go anytime though. This motivates me to work hard every day.

With this kind of job, you become very good at it once you've worked here for a long time. And if you're ambitious, you can study more and get more training, take a test to get certified or licensed to work in different departments for higher-paying jobs and chances for promotion. I'm 50 already so I'm satisfied with the job I have now. Of course, if I were younger, I'd pursue higher education and get a better job. When I was younger, I didn't have the opportunity to go to a university in Vietnam because my father was in the army for the South. It was my misfortune, but my younger brother went to university, and he's been very successful.

Education is very important. I tell my sons that all the time. I hope that they can go to school when they come to the US. My sons are still young, they can study and get a good education so they'll have better jobs in the future. I don't know what they want to do, I can't force them or speak for them, I just want them not to have to live the life their mom did. It's not a bad life, but it's an unfulfilled one.

Houston, July 2011
Ngoc-Diep Tang

artist

Hello, my name's Trịnh Cung and I was born in 1939. I've been an artist for more than 40 years now. I work with oil paints. I grew up in Nha Trang. In high school, I hated maths and science but loved poetry, literature, and especially art. For me, art was the freedom to feel, to love, to enter into the movement of life itself. So after I graduated, I begged my parents to let me go to Huế and try to get into the Fine Arts College there. Huế is a wonderland, you know? The Hương River, the beautiful landscapes, the atmosphere of the old capital .... There are so many wonderful artists and poets that came from Huế, like Hàn Mặc Tử and Xuân Diệu. So I followed my heart and went to Huế.

Anyway, there were a hundred applicants for admission to the College and only 15 places. For the admission test, they just put a statue in front of all of us and told us to draw it. Simple, right? As I was drawing, I kept looking around at everyone's drawings, and they were really good. Compared to theirs, mine looked like shit. I asked some people how they were able to draw so well and they told me they'd been practicing and taking art lessons privately. I thought there was no way in hell I was going to get in. After the exam, I just packed up and got ready to go home.

When some people told me I'd gotten in, I thought they were kidding. They told me to go see for myself. I ran to the college to the notice board where they'd posted the results and there was my name! I couldn't believe it ... I was so excited!

In the College, they didn't teach us any modern art. In fact, they hated modern art. We were forbidden to paint in any style except classical realism. There were some students who tried to paint in a modern style but they got kicked out. I had no desire to get kicked out, so at school I did what I was told and emulated all the old masters, but at home I experimented with modern art. My inspiration was artists like Picasso, Chagall, Van Gogh, Gauguin, Matisse, Kandinsky, Klee, Pollack, and Modigliani. Modern art was so new and exciting for us artists. For a lot of us, it was representative of the kinds of change we wanted to see in what was, back then, still a very conservative society.

I really grew as an artist during my four years at the College. Out of the 15 students who got in that year, only one or two of us went on to become well-known artists. I put it all down to creativity. The first step in learning to paint is easy: you learn to copy. The next step is the hard one: communicating what you feel. It's easy enough to teach a student to paint a portrait; the student just has to copy what they see. What can't be taught is how to put soul and feeling onto the canvas. A good painting should be alive; it should communicate happiness, sadness, even memory.

After I graduated from the College, the first painting that really got me noticed was called "Mùa Thu Tuổi Nhỏ" [Children's Autumn]. Back in 1962, they organized an exhibition in Saigon that featured the best works of 21 different artists from around the world. There were artists from Germany, France, England, Spain …. And there I was, just barely out of Art College and exhibiting along with all these international artists. I was really proud. I don't have the painting any more though. It was sold to a woman living in Washington, DC.

I always knew that I wanted to be an artist and that art was my true passion. Being an artist isn't easy though. Take Van Gogh, for example. He had a hard and lonely life. He couldn't sell any paintings during his lifetime and died young and penniless. It was only after he died that people began to appreciate his work. But thanks to his dedication to his art, he'll be remembered forever.

As an artist, I've done well for myself. My paintings aren't expensive but they're not exactly cheap either. The price really depends on the size. A medium-sized canvas can range from

$3,000 to $5,000 while a large canvas can cost up to $10,000. It's not all about the size though. The price also depends on how much I like my painting. It's harder for me to let go of a painting if I really love it. On the other hand, if I don't like it, I trash it; I'll only sell works I'm satisfied with. In an average year I probably do about 10 paintings; multiply that by 40 years and it makes 400 or so paintings over my lifetime.

My art has changed a lot since I first started painting, but especially over the last 15 years or so. Up until 1996 I painted only figurative art. You could always tell what my painting was about: a woman, a place, an object, whatever. Then in 1996 I was invited to San Francisco State University as a guest lecturer. While I was there, I was able to visit a lot of different museums, not just in the Bay Area but also other museums like the Museum Of Modern Art in New York and the Museum Of Contemporary Art in LA. The experience really inspired me. I began to experiment more with my art. I began painting much more abstractly.

Success can be a real problem for an artist. It's important to remember that just because people are clapping doesn't mean they actually like your work. Once you forget this, you begin to fear any sort of criticism, you become afraid to take risks. It happens all the time. An artist sells a painting and then they feel like they have no choice but to continue painting the same thing. They're afraid that if they don't, the applause will stop. Eventually, they turn into a forgery of themselves. And that is the death of an artist.

Saigon, October 2011
Mai Quang Huy, Colleen Thuy-Tien Ngo, Josh Mayhew, Mai Lan

art forger

I started doing this part-time while I was still a student at the University of Industrial Arts. My major was actually Applied Art: I studied forming and shaping things like propellers, car parts, whatever, as long as they could be shaped and then used in industry. But somehow I ended up working part-time for some art forgery shops in the Old Quarter. Now I have my own shop. Altogether, ever since my third year of college, I've been in the business for 14 or 15 years.

I've had this shop in the Old Quarter for four years now. The rent here costs a fortune: 20 million đồng [$1,000] per month. So I'm always telling myself to try harder. If I don't have enough customers, I won't have enough orders. And without enough orders I can't hire many painters, which means less profit. Vietnamese buy mostly around Tết or other big holidays, and foreigners buy during the tourist season. Anytime there's a drop in the number of tourists, like when we had the SARS crisis a few years ago, it can be a real struggle just to pay the rent.

I've got five painters working for me right now. They make between 3 and 4 million đồng [$150–$200] a month, depending on how good they are. I've got some that are really ineffective: even though they're always painting, they never seem to finish anything. Then there are the ones who get their work done and wait for me to give them more.

A forger has to be experienced, and to know something about the work they're going to copy. They have to know the language, the way to mix the colors, the way to make the brushstrokes, what to paint first and what to paint next. Forgers tend to be better at some styles than at others: one person may be good at Classicalism, another may be good at Surrealism. Even if there's no real standard, still, a professional can always look at a painting and tell if the forger has reached a certain level or if they've really grasped the painting's spirit.

We get all sorts of customers: foreigners and locals. Some people just buy for fun, others buy because they like a particular painting, and some people, especially foreigners, buy paintings to resell when they get home. The price of a painting depends on a lot of things: the size of the painting, the technical difficulty involved, the time a painter spends on it, etc. Labor is cheap in Vietnam though, so a painting that costs $35 or $40 here could cost $1,000 or more if you bought it in the West.

We do every kind of painting: any artist, any time period, any style. And now that Vietnamese are becoming more aware of art, there's more demand for work by local artists. Most of our paintings are ready-made: the customer just walks in and buys a painting off the shelf.

But we also do made-to-order works. Some customers may commission us to do a painting that they're particularly fond of. Then there are others who want us to do a painting based on a photo of their family or a pet. We also get a lot of photographers who want to recreate their photos in the language of painting. Then they sell the paintings as their own artwork. If they respect us, they'll let the painters sign their names, but that hardly ever happens.

Running a business like this is hard work. There have been times when I've thought I should follow my major and go back to designing things, but somehow I could never bring myself to spend all day in an office staring at a computer screen. I guess forgery is just a better fit for me. Even if I don't have time now to follow my own passions and create my own art, sometimes in life, passion has to take a backseat to more everyday concerns. For now, I'm still lucky to have a job that gives me freedom and allows me a broad perspective on life.

Hanoi, November 2010
Jesse Van Fleet, Đinh Hà Thu, Kristine Nguyen, Mary Luc, Nguyễn Phương Chi

film director

My name is Đỗ Minh Tuấn and I'm a film director. Over the years I've directed a lot of films and television programs. You might know some of them: Vua Bãi Rác [Garbage Dump King], Ký Ức Điện Biên [Memories of Điện Biên Phủ], and the TV series Bí Mật Eva [Eve's Secret].

I graduated from Hanoi National University in 1975. I'd started out studying geology, but after several years I found my real calling and graduated with a degree in literature. I think I inherited my passion for the arts from my parents. They exposed me to a wide range of books and magazines while I was growing up. I was also really lucky that they understood my need for freedom. They always let me make my own decisions and follow the path of my own choosing.

After I graduated, I worked for the Institute of Philosophy in Hanoi for a bit [*laughs*]. Even though I love poetry, literature, and the arts, for a while I had to put them aside for my left hand while my right hand concentrated on the sciences. It was when I was working at the Philosophy Institute that I first thought of directing films. I don't know exactly when, but at some point

I started to feel that my life needed a change; I needed to do something creative. So I quit my job and started taking courses at the Hanoi University of Drama and Cinematography. I graduated in 1986 and came to work at the Vietnam Feature Film Studio. I've been working here ever since.

Working at the State film studio forces you to ... well, let's just say I have to follow orders [*laughs*]. I'm a creative guy, but sometimes I have to bottle up my creativity. Luckily, I've still got ways to keep my productions from being censored too much. For example, sometimes they check my screenplay and they ask me to alter it. No problem! So I change the screenplay, but when I'm filming, I still do it the way I want [*laughs*]. When they figure out what happened, I just explain that it's all part of the process of making films — sometimes the screenplay and the actual film just end up being different. Other times I tell them that I accept the changes they're suggesting, and then do nothing. But then they also do nothing ... [*shrugs*]. Maybe the censors forget what they told me to change, or maybe they think that telling me is enough and they've done their job. Maybe they don't want to make it any more difficult for me ... I don't know.

One of my favorite anecdotes is when the censors wanted me to change the name of the film Vua Bãi Rác [Garbage Dump King]. They felt that the name implied Vietnam was a garbage dump and that the film would "destroy the image of the nation." I pretended to change the name but then I snuck it into the title sequence of the final version [*smiles*]. By that time, there was no money left to make any changes, so I got to keep the name after all [*laughs*].

Vua Bãi Rác was one of the most successful films of my career. You could even call it one of the most famous films to come out of Vietnam. It was really well received at several international film festivals, and it was even supposed to be on the list of foreign films to be nominated for an Oscar. Unfortunately, our submission was late and in the end we couldn't get it onto the list. Altogether, my films have been shown in more than 40 film festivals around the world.

Another thing I'm really proud of is when I was offered a fellowship to study at the William Joiner Center for the Study of War and Social Consequences. Thanks to this fellowship, I was able to spend several months in California researching the Vietnamese community there. I ended up writing a lot of articles about Vietnamese culture abroad. I also had the opportunity to attend film festivals and market my films. That was when I started working on my very first English screenplay, titled "The Monkey King." But when I got back to Vietnam, I found myself too busy with other work and my point of view towards China changed. These days I'm thinking about working on a project about Vietnamese around the world.

My life inspires my art. Even though I already have a completed screenplay in my hand, I'll suddenly see a sun ray or feel a gust of wind that inspires me and I'll just go after it; I try to catch it and then end up totally changing the screenplay [*laughs*]. I like to think that's why audiences can share my every emotion and every idea … they cry and laugh and they laugh and cry along with the characters in my films. Of course, working like this can get me into trouble with production managers, the kind of trouble that has affected my promotion …. But if I could turn back the clock, I'd still do it all over again. If I had a chance to meet myself 30 years ago, I'd only have two pieces of advice: first, go to the US sooner; second, buy an iPad [*laughs*].

These days I'm a kind of jack of all trades: poet, writer, playwright, artist, film director, and philosopher. Keeping busy and stimulating my creativity has always been the key to my success. I'm 59 now, so according to the law they have to put me out to pasture next year. But for me, retirement means nothing.

Right now, I'm working on "Adam's Secret," a spin-off of my TV series "Eve's Secret." I'm also writing a new screenplay about Trần Hưng Đạo [a thirteenth-century hero], rewriting some of my old screenplays, preparing for a festival in Đà Nẵng, and putting the finishing touches on an upcoming exhibition of my artwork. Art is my life. The day I leave art will be the day I leave this life.

Hanoi, November 2011
Colleen Thuy-Tien Ngo, Mai Lan, Josh Mayhew, Mai Quang Huy

chapter 6

SELLING

flower seller

My name is Yến. I'm 40 years old, and I work as a flower seller at Mơ market. This is my third job and I've been doing this for 10 years. Before this, I worked for a construction company for 16 years until it went bankrupt. At first, I went back to farming in the countryside. Then, after awhile, I started selling flowers in Hanoi.

Every day, I get up at 4 a.m. to buy flowers wholesale from a good friend at Mai Dịch market. On a normal day, I buy around 250 to 300 flowers, but on holidays like the first and middle of the Lunar month, Teachers' Day, Valentine's Day, or Women's Day, I can buy anywhere between 600 to 700 flowers. Then, I ride to the Mơ market with the baskets of flowers. I used to cycle around Mơ market selling flowers from the back of my bicycle because mobile selling was incredibly efficient. The flowers would sell out fast. But these days, I just sell them from my spot under this tree. Sometimes business is really slow and the hours just drag by.

On an average day I make around a 60,000 đồng [$3] profit, so that means about 1.8 million [$90] a month. That's just enough to cover the basic living expenses for my family. I've got two kids: the first one is already married, and my second girl is in her last year at university. She's got a part-time job selling cigarettes so I don't have to pay her tuition.

If I compare myself to other flower sellers, I make less money because I always charge the same price no matter who you are. I figure this is the best way for me to keep my old customers and attract new ones. Really, I get customers from all walks of life. But if I had to break it down, I'd have to say that a lot of my customers are housewives. Then there are the older people who buy flowers for the beginning and middle of the lunar month, and the young professionals who want flowers to decorate the office. I don't get many people buying flowers to give as gifts, or for weddings or other ceremonies — that's when people go to a flower shop instead.

Roses are my bestsellers because they're cheap and you can use them for almost every occasion. I also sell lilies, mums, and moon flowers. Of course at Tết, I sell a lot of peach branches and peach trees. I buy them wholesale at Nhật Tân in the weeks before the New Year, and sell them right up to the day before. The increased profits go to helping me prepare to celebrate Tết with my own family. I usually take a week off to spend time at home and then I go back to work on the sixth day of the New Year.

There are things that I like and things I don't like about my job. I like the control that being self-employed gives me. I can stay home when I'm sick, when the weather's bad, or when I've got family business to attend to — no need to ask the boss for permission. Plus, the start-up costs are low and the job doesn't require any special skills or training.

On the other hand, working with flowers is really hard on your hands — by the end of the day, my hands are covered with cuts from handling the roses. And while this job may give me a lot of freedom, the downside is that my income is dependent

on factors outside my control. I remember rainy days when I considered myself lucky for having sold just three flowers. And the day after a heavy rain, the wholesale price of flowers skyrockets and it's hard for me to make a profit. Or there are the times when someone's chosen their flowers and I've wrapped them up, all ready to go, only to have the customer realize they left their money at home. Sometimes I really wonder whether this job is worth it.

Last, I don't like the way the government's economic renovation policies have labelled occupations like mine "illegal." Especially in the last few years, the cops have really started to make trouble. They make it seem like I'm some sort of problem that needs to be fixed. They sweep through the neighborhood five times a day. Often, they'll make me move my business, and several times they've confiscated my bicycle. If I want it back, I have to pay 100,000 đồng [$5]. That's more money than I make in a day, but without my bicycle how am I supposed to work?

I've been selling flowers at Mơ market for 10 years now. But ever since they tore down the old market and replaced it with this new shopping center, my business has slowed down a lot. I wish I had the money to open my own flower shop, but the way things are going these days, that's just a dream.

So I'll just keep selling my flowers under this tree in front of Mơ market until I get old. Even if this job is hard sometimes, just knowing that my flowers can bring joy to the lives of my customers and their family and friends still means a lot to me.

Hanoi, October 2010
Nguyễn Hương Lan, Nguyễn Phương Vân, Son Chau, Micaela Bacon,
Lena Tran

fish seller

My name is Giang, I'm 45 years old, and I've been an ornamental fish peddler for ten years now. I quit school in seventh grade. After that, I worked as a laborer for a state-owned construction company. Then ten years ago, I quit and started selling ornamental fish.

Basically, my day consists of wandering the streets selling fish in plastic bags. In the morning, I put fish in big and medium-sized bags of water. I use a pump to fill the bags with oxygen or else the fish will die. Then I load the bags on my bicycle, and ride to wherever in the city I think I can sell them. I stop to rest when I'm tired, and only come back home after the afternoon rush hour.

I raise some of my fish myself, the others I purchase. My hometown in Nam Định is where my fish "workshop" is. I only keep a small number of fish here in Hanoi. I pay 1 million [$50] a month to rent a 15 square meter house in Gia Lâm. I live there alone, without my wife and kids, because most of the space is taken up by my stuff and the fish tanks. My wife stays home to work on the farm and take care of the fish. I go home twice a year to help with the rice harvest. I go for about 20 days each time. Other than that, I just go home for the Tết holidays.

The total number of customers changes every day. Parents tend to buy more in the summertime when their kids are off for summer vacation and have more time to play with the fish. Sometimes I get rich families who buy fish that can cost several million đồng [$100 or more]. When that happens, I'll deliver the fish to their homes. If they need more, I'll get them from Nam Định. When I don't have what I need here, I call home to ask someone to send the fish by bus or small truck. This is one of the conveniences I can offer my customers: immediate, personalized service. Other than fish and fish food, I also provide tanks and water filtration systems, but I don't carry that sort of stuff with me during the day. Customers have to order in advance, and I'll deliver them another day.

To do this job, you need good weather conditions. It's hard to sell if it's really hot and almost impossible when it's too cold or rainy. During the winter, you can't do much but stay home. It can be hard sometimes, but there aren't that many difficulties. The fish rarely get sick, and when they do, you just have to deal with it. After all, it's your job. The thing I hate most about this job is the way the streets these days are full of dust and pollution. Also, sometimes the local police hassle me and try and make me leave the area. One time they actually fined me 150,000 đồng [$7.50].

But when I get a steady stream of customers, life can be pretty good. I put in 20 million đồng [$1,000] when I started out. In an average month these days, I make about 5 or 6 million [$250-$300]. I can live on that. And besides, at this age, I can't really switch careers. The only thing I could do to make things easier would be to rent a shop. But that's expensive: anywhere from 5 to 7 million đồng [$250–$350] a month.

Now, while I'm still in good health, I'm just focusing on supporting our family and paying for our kids' education. Right now, both our kids are in college. The younger one is in her first year of college, studying pre-school education, and my son is studying to work in the oil industry. I hope they can pursue their course of study after college and not end up following in their dad's footsteps. As for me, I'll just keep doing what I'm doing. After all, I like my job — it's fun, and it's nice to be able to spend the day taking care of my fish!

Hanoi, November 2010
Đinh Hà Thu, Kristine Nguyen, Mary Luc, Nguyễn Phương Chi,
Jesse Van Fleet

adult store salesperson

I'm a third-year college student studying accounting at the College of Transportation. I was looking for a job through some online job postings and the adult store company contacted me. When I went to drop off my resume, I was really concerned that the shop was so far away and the commute would be really inconvenient. The first time they called me for an interview, I didn't go. Then they called me again the next day. They sounded so enthusiastic that I decided to go in the end.

So that's how I ended up as an accountant and sales assistant at an adult store. During the two month probation period, I received 80 per cent of the regular salary. The job was all right, so I continued working. But to tell you the truth, I thought this job was disgraceful in the beginning. I really didn't expect to see so many women and well-educated people come into the shop. But everyone is young and really dynamic. And the working environment is good too.

When I first started working here, I didn't even know what "adult store" meant. In my whole life, I'd never even seen or touched a condom. Seriously, it wasn't until I worked here that I understood what a condom was. If they had put me in this sales position right after I joined the company, I probably wouldn't have accepted it. But I got used to it after working for a while in telephone sales where no one knew who I was. Gradually, I became more open about the job and wasn't embarrassed anymore.

These days, my job is simply to sell things to the customers who come into the shop. I don't have to go out and find customers like a pharmaceutical company sales rep, for example. Every day, I get about five to seven walk-in customers and they only stay for five or ten minutes each. When they come in, I ask them what they're looking for and what their preferences are so I can help them find suitable products. It's pretty simple, really. I just study the information on the back of the packaging so I can introduce the products to the customers.

Most of the customers who come in already use these kinds of products. They'll ask which item is the best or the most popular, and I'll help them choose some. For example, they'll ask if we have condoms that have spikes, that are slim, that are made in England, Japan, or America .... If a woman tells me, for example, "My boyfriend performs poorly or has premature ejaculation," then I'll help her boyfriend by bringing out the right products. They'll bring it home to try it, if it works for them they'll continue using it, if it doesn't, then they can try something else.

Usually, there are more men than women coming in, and more young adults than middle-aged people. But when middle-aged people come in, they buy more products. Our oldest customer is like, 45 years old or something. The youngest were probably these two girls who were in their first year of college who came in to buy stuff for their parents.

A lot of customers ask if I'm married yet and I have to lie and say that I am. If I don't, a lot of them will tease me or try to seduce me. That's why when you're selling stuff like this, you have to be determined, more serious, and cannot flirt or laugh. In general, though, I feel like men who use condoms are more civilized. They're considerate of their girlfriend and of other people in society. That's why I'm enthusiastic about my work and introducing our products to people.

The thing I like about this job is the light workload. I work exactly eight hours a day. I go to college at night, so I need this kind of arrangement. If I didn't get that, I'd never work here — the salary is too low. But the good thing is my boss never pressures me or gives me any trouble. He's really easygoing. He works the night shift; when he comes in, I just tell him if anything is sold out. Otherwise, he never worries about the shop or checks on me during the day.

Everyone tells me it's my fate to be in sales. Before this, I sold paintings for five or six hours a day and I got 1.8 million đồng [$90]. Here, I work eight hours and get 1.5 million [$75]. So if my boss ever does get harder on me, I'll probably quit; the hours are just too long and the salary is too low.

Sometimes I do get a bit embarrassed about working here. Some of my friends know what I do, but I tell everyone else I sell medicinal foods, not condoms. My parents back in my hometown in Nam Định still don't know. And if people back home in the village ever found out I was selling condoms, I'd never hear the end of it. Even my boyfriend doesn't like me working here. But really, why should it matter? I'm not doing anything bad. It's just a job. I'm just making a living for myself.

Hanoi, October 2010
Irene Van, Nguyễn Thái Linh, Sharon Seegers, Vũ Hoàng An

car dealer

I've been crazy about cars ever since I was a little kid. My training is actually in IT, but seven years ago I decided to follow my passion and get into the car business. Initially, I sold cars wholesale and retail, then I opened this showroom with a group of good friends. We've been in business for three years now.

We weren't the first to open a car showroom in Hanoi, so from the start we've avoided the low and mid-range of the market. Instead, we provide high-end products for high-end customers. This means we take a completely different approach compared to your average car dealership, where customers worry about things like loans or depreciation or fuel efficiency. Basically, rich people just want a car that shows off their position. Do you really think someone who buys a Rolls Royce cares about the price of fuel?

I love my job because I get to work with technology and speed. We don't focus on one particular brand at my showroom. Sometimes, we bring in cars from ten different brands in one month. Some of the brands we're selling right now are Rolls Royce, Bentley, Lexus, Mercedes, BMW, you name it. For each brand I do thorough research to see what the best features of the different cars are. I'm passionate about these things. But as for myself, I've just got a normal small car for going to work and back. It's a Toyota Yaris, which goes for about $45,000 in Vietnam.

There are a lot of obstacles to doing this type of business in Vietnam, but the biggest one is taxes. The cars we sell are already not cheap. For example, a Rolls Royce in America costs about $300,000. But with import duties and luxury taxes, in Vietnam the exact same car will cost close to $1 million. There are several reasons for the high taxes. For one, transportation infrastructure in Vietnam is still underdeveloped, so the government wants to discourage car use. At the same time, the government wants to encourage the growth of local manufacturing by increasing the cost of foreign cars. Aside from taxes, the government is also regulating car sales more and more. There's a new policy [Decree 20 of the Ministry of Industry and Trade] enacted this year that requires importers to have the permission of the manufacturer. Plus, they're trying to hold us to specific standards for service and warranties. I'm still able to bend the rules, but it's getting more difficult.

I can count on my fingers the number of showrooms that sell cars like this in Hanoi — the initial investment is just too high. For example, imagine this: a car costs $300,000, plus the $600,000 in taxes. The tax on one car alone can get you a nice house. So where do we get the money to have cars on the showroom floor? The only way we can do business is by taking out loans from the bank, but a lot of other shops don't have that luxury. Instead, they have to pay $300,000 to buy 30 cheap cars. Their margin is smaller, but they have a higher turnover.

So basically, I'm a middleman. I buy cars in the US, import them to Vietnam, and then sell them. If I were a car dealer in the US there would be limits to the margin I could charge. For example, in the US, if the manufacturer sells the car to the dealer at $120,000, then the dealer is limited to a certain maximum price, say, no more than $130,000. As for me, I only care about the market in Vietnam. If there's an oversupply of cars in Vietnam then the price is lower; the price is higher if they're scarce. Overall, though, the government's import restrictions mean that the supply of cars can't meet the demand. So any dealer with the inventory can increase their prices. That's just how the market works.

The weird thing is that in Vietnam people don't finance their cars like they do in other countries. Here, people just pay the full amount at once; if they need to borrow money, they'll do it through their bank and then wire us the money. You can either pay in cash or with a wire. Usually people wire us the money, but we do have some customers who pay in cash. Sometimes people try to pay with US dollars, but that's actually against the law.

We focus on the high-end market, so all the recent inflation hasn't affected us too much. That said, sales are slower this year compared to last year. Two years ago, sales were really good; on average we sold seven cars per week. Now, there are times when we only sell one per month. It's the same with other dealers in town.

Our customers are all Vietnamese. Foreigners are more practical-minded; they don't need to show off with a fancy car. Plus, foreigners who work here have the option of importing any car they want tax-free as long as it's for personal use and they send it back home when they're done working in Vietnam. Our average customer has as many as three luxury cars. It's not like they drive their Rolls Royce to go to the market: they own different cars for different purposes.

Most of our customers are from Hanoi, but we also have customers who come from the provinces. Actually, we prefer the customers from the provinces because they tend to have researched the car they like really thoroughly before they come to the showroom. Once they get here, if the car's in stock, they buy it immediately. Customers from Hanoi are more work: they shop around a lot before they decide to buy.

We also have some customers who're gangsters. You can tell just by looking at them — you know, tattoos all over their bodies, and big thick gold chains. These kinds of customers have a lot of cash, so if they like the car they'll buy it right away. But they also might turn around and sell it the next day. We don't really want to get too close to these customers, but sometimes they can bring us benefits regular customers can't. Say, for example, some local mafia comes into the showroom and demands protection money for us to stay open. That's when knowing some "special customers" can come in handy to solve little problems like that [laughs].

Honestly, you don't really need a lot of training to do well at this job. It's all about salesmanship. You just have to be able to steer the customers to the cars we've got in the shop at the moment. For example, if a customer says they want to buy a certain car that we don't have, I have to somehow convince them to buy a car we do have. If I'm good, they'll change their mind and buy the car we've got. Not everyone can do that. To tell you the

truth, I'm not that good at it, but luckily for me, a lot of my staff
are [*laughs*].

Hanoi, November 2011
Ngoc-Diep Tang, Hoàng Huyền Trang, Haven Rocha, Vũ Phương Thảo

promotion girl

If you want to be a promotion girl, you've got to be good-
looking and tall, at least 160 cm. Me, I'm 167 cm tall. But your
appearance is only a small part of it; you've also got to be clever
and persuasive, and know how to interact with people. And these
days a lot of events attract customers from different countries,
so it's a big plus if a promotion girl knows foreign languages.
Really, success in this day and age is all about knowledge. Even as
a promotion girl, you still need more than just your looks if you
want to get ahead.

Most recently, I worked at a motor show at the Giảng Võ
Convention Center that lasted for six days. There were two
shifts: from 8:30 a.m. to 2:30 p.m. and 2:30 p.m. to 8:30 p.m. I
chose the first shift. My job was to stand in front of the cars and
introduce them to the customers. I was supposed to answer any
questions they had. That means that in addition to standing next
to the cars and letting people take pictures of me, I also had to
know something about the cars themselves. Everybody thinks that
being a promotion girl is so simple: just stand there and make the
product look good. But it's not like that at all. For example even

when the weather's cold like this, we still have to stand there in our thin little outfits and our 10 cm heels with the air conditioners blasting out cold air. After a while your legs are killing you! And no matter how tired you get you can't show it, you still have to smile for the customers and answer whatever questions they ask. And sometimes, they ask a lot of questions!

Actually, the motor show was my first real promotional event. Before that, I only worked at conferences, events at hotels, stuff like that, where they needed people who could speak foreign languages. So when I worked at the motor show, I was shocked. Before that, I only had to stand for two hours and then I could take a break. But at the motor show, I had to stand for way longer. I was so tired! But I'd already taken the job, so I had to do it. They paid me 300,000 đồng [$15] a shift. I know to most people that sounds like a lot of money, but that's only because they don't know how hard we have to work. That's why I say that promotion girls who've gone to school and can speak foreign languages are going to get better gigs with higher salaries. If all you can do is stand there and look pretty, you're not going to make much at all. I've promised myself that I'm never going to work at another promotional event like that again.

Of course, working at the motor show I got to learn a lot of new things about cars. It was really cool. But I still prefer to work at conferences because I can get to know more people and build up my social network. And I still have the opportunity to learn new things. The best is working at an event where a company is introducing electronics or cars, for example. There are many things I would never have learned if I didn't work as a promotion girl.

I'm super busy with school and work, but I've learned ways to cope. It's okay to neglect schoolwork sometimes — you can make up for it later — but I can feel my friendships fading away because I've got no time to hang out with my friends anymore. Honestly, I know I've lost many things I cannot gain back. But right now, I'm trying to gain some of them back. That's another reason why I'm working fewer hours now: so I have more time with my friends.

You face a lot of challenges working as a promotion girl. The biggest one is the way we're exposed to bad influences. In this line of work it's really easy to meet "powerful men" [đại gia, the reference is to the opportunity to become a mistress]. Secondly, we're college students and it's easy to lose sight of the fact that our main goal should be studying. The salary is high and the work is easy; if we're not careful we'll let our studies slide. Next is the way some customers treat us. Of course, in society these days, people like this aren't that common; most people understand that promotion girls don't just stand there looking pretty, but can actually be an important part of a product's success. But girls who have to dress more "sexy," like the promotion girls who work for Vinagame, for example, may be exposed to inappropriate comments or behavior. Of course, I've never accepted work like that. And I know some girls will even provide additional "services." I don't know much about it, but it probably happens. But every job has its good and bad sides, you know?

The maximum working age for a promotion girl is 25 years old. Firstly, being a promotion girl is a temporary job; you do it if it fits your needs at a certain point in your life. After that, a promotion girl might move into management or go into a completely different line of work. I never for a second considered making this my career, I only did it to build my confidence and gain new experiences. Right now, I'm studying Korean. After I graduate, I want to work first as a translator, and then study Marketing. My plan is to work for companies that organize events. You know, as a PR manager. I might still participate in events, but just to facilitate. Honestly, money was only one factor when I decided to work as a promotion girl; for me the important things were gaining experience and confidence. And now I can say I'm a confident person; I could never say that before.

Hanoi, November 2010
Truong Minh Giang, Mai Nguyen, Carol Nguyen, John Tran, Đỗ Thu Huong

chapter 7

MANAGING

homemaker

Hello everyone, my name is Thúy and I'm 45 years old. Right
now, I'm living happily with my husband and two kids. I'm very
lucky to have a boy and a girl. My boy is 13 and in eighth grade,
and my youngest is 8 and in third grade. Now I'm working a job
that doesn't have a name [*laughs*]. Just kidding, I don't have a
job; instead, I devote my day to my little family, and I know a lot
of women like that. You think staying at home all day means my
hands and feet aren't put to use? If you think that, you don't know
what it's like to be a mother [*laughs*]!

My husband and I have a beautiful relationship. We were in
love for ten years and lived together before getting married. At
the time, everyone teased me about being too picky and giving
my old man Phúc — my husband's name is Phúc — a hard time
by making him wait [*laughs*]. But when I was young, I had a lot
of dreams and ambitions, I wanted to explore more, I didn't want
to get married and have kids early. So I only got married in 1995,
when I was 29 years old. Three years later, I had my first child.

People often say that I should've been a man because I've got a
strong sense of determination and I always do what I say. I always
try my best but sometimes things just don't work out as planned.
When I was in high school, I wanted to go to a university. My
dream was the National Economics University. I still remember
the afternoon when my best friend and I were walking around
the lake, and over the community loudspeaker system they
started reading out the entrance score requirements for the annual
university entrance exam. As I listened to the results, I froze. I'd
gotten 13.5, and the entrance score was 14. I'd missed by half a
point.

I was sad for the rest of the day. The thought that I'd failed
by just half a point kept going round and round in my head.
But I decided not to dwell on it, and I asked my parents to give
me another year to study to pass the exam. The extra year might
mean I could fulfill my dream of going to university, but even if it
didn't, it would be a chance to try my best and have no regrets. Do
you understand? I mean, it was my last chance. If I passed, I would
be a serious student. And if I failed, I wouldn't give it a second
thought, I'd find a suitable job and work hard at it. You know
what I mean? If you know you've given it all you've got, you can
feel comfortable and accept the truth, even if it's a sad truth.

And the result was … I still failed [*laughs*]. You want to
know if I was sad? I'd be lying if I said no. But if you ask me if I
regretted it, then no, I felt like a weight had been lifted from my
shoulders and I accepted the result. Maybe I'm not fated to study
in a university environment but I can keep studying in the school
of life. That's how I motivate myself [*laughs*].

My first job was at a wood processing plant. The plant made
a lot of different products, from wooden toys to massage tables;
sometimes we received custom orders for specific products. I
worked there for three years, from 1986 to 1989. Then I took a

training course so I could work in the music conservatory making and fixing the instruments. I remember the time I won the "golden hands" award for my work. It came with a gift of 100,000 đồng [$5]. These days that doesn't sound like much, but at that time 100,000 đồng was a lot of money.

Then in 1995, I married my husband. At the time, my husband's family was very poor, and I knew that if I married him we couldn't expect to depend on his family. But I loved him and wanted to live with him. It made my heart ache to watch him struggle by himself. My husband is a man of honesty and integrity. I love his character and his honesty, but more than that, I love him because he's faithful in the love he gives me. And on top of it all, he's also a very handy guy, and enthusiastic too. That's why our neighbors always ask him for help, to fix a door, build a table, solder this, weld that … sometimes he's really busy helping the neighbors, and I feel for him [laughs].

In 2003, I was still weak four months after giving birth to my youngest child. I considered leaving my job. I thought about it a lot because I still loved my job. You know, my manager would even call me sometimes, asking me when I was going to come back to work. I thought about it for a long time. If I went back to work, I could make some extra money. Of course, I didn't want to put the entire financial burden on my husband. But my kids were still young — one was starting primary school, the other was just a few months old — and my in-laws were too old to take care of them. I knew they needed me. If my husband and I spent a lot of time working, they wouldn't feel the love of a family. I don't want my kids to grow up like that!

I talked with my husband about it and he encouraged me to stay home to take care of our kids and my health. He would try his best to support our family. He told me not to worry so much. He said that he would be less worried if he knew that I was at home to take care of our family. Thanks to his support, I finally made up my mind to stay at home and take care of our two kids.

Luckily, my little princess was pretty easy to raise so I wasn't that tired. At first, I was so bored and didn't know what to do besides work around the house. I was kind of a workaholic; I always worked efficiently with a schedule and saved up a lot of free time. That's why I still had spare time when others usually didn't. I thought that I could still work at home even though I couldn't work outside. To make the most of my time while Hoàng was at kindergarten and Hà was sleeping, I made and embroidered shoes. It didn't make much money but I wanted to help my husband in any way I could.

At the time, we still lived in a very small, dark house on a corner; it was only 22 meters square. So I decided to redecorate our house. The first reason was to make us feel more comfortable in our own house, and the second reason was to make guests feel welcome. I talked with my husband about it and he supported me completely. I painted the house with brighter colors, bought a new wardrobe, new furniture and a new cupboard. Everything was small, to match our little house. Then I bought some small flower pots for the porch and guest room. The house looked completely different! And I noticed a change in my husband's mood: when he came home from work, he smiled more than usual. I like to think our beautiful and tidy home made him want to come and stay home more.

All day long, I look forward to seeing my husband and my kids; then we'll sit, have dinner, and talk together. I always try to make dishes that my husband and kids love; it makes me happy to see them have a nice meal. Cooking good food for the family is the pride and happiness of any mother, you know? My husband and my kids love each other so much, when I see them playing and smiling together, I feel so happy that my time at home alone suddenly disappears. I'm also the emotional type; I cry easily when I'm alone at home, missing my husband and kids [*laughs*].

Heaven never ignores those who try their best. After a few years, my husband inherited a 200 square meter plot from his parents. We built a brand new 60 square meter house. We mainly used our savings; the rest we borrowed from relatives. Now, when I learned we were going to build a new house, I immediately thought about building a guest house because the demand for renting rooms was very high at that time. And I was right! Now we have 15 rooms for rent, and they're all filled. There are 5 rooms for families and 10 smaller rooms mainly for students.

Now, besides taking care of our house, I take care of the rooms for rent. My kids are on break from school now so I also have to give them work to do. It seems easy when I put it this way, but it actually keeps me very busy! In the morning, my husband takes the kids to school and then goes to work. I also wake up early and go to the market to buy groceries for the day. I spend most of the morning cleaning the house and doing the laundry. Luckily, we have more money now so we managed to buy a washing machine — what a relief for me!

At noon, my husband comes home and has lunch with me while the kids have lunch at school. This is the time when my husband and I share our opinions and feelings, and discuss plans for our future. I always appreciate these moments because we have this time to understand and love each other more [*smiles*]. In the afternoon, I visit the rental rooms to check if everything's okay and listen to the tenants' feedback. Sometimes, I visit my neighbors just to check in on them. One time they complained about a young renter who always made a lot of noise with his motorbike when going through the alley. After that, I went home and handled it. I have a responsibility to bridge differences between our tenants and neighbors so that everyone is happy and comfortable.

Now I worry most about my two kids. They are both in school so I try to create the best environment for them to study in. Nowadays we don't have as many difficulties as we had in the past, so we can save money and invest it for our son and daughter. I want them to study hard so they can find jobs that they love and that contribute to society.

I know that in Vietnam these days, there are a lot of women who don't want to sacrifice their career for family. But you have to look at the positives of this choice too. Look at me: I'm completely satisfied with my life right now, satisfied with my job without a name. For me, a woman can find her success in building a happy home with her husband and kids. In this day and age, women can do anything we want, we can become doctors, engineers, whatever, and work until we retire, but building a happy family is a job we can do all our lives!

Hanoi, November 2011
Michelle Ta, Ngô Mai Hương, Tina Thy Pham, Nguyễn Hà Phương Ninh

deputy director of strategy

My name is Thảo, I'm 25 years old, and I'm the Deputy General Director of Strategy for Phạm Nguyên Foods. Our company is the second largest producer of choco pies in Vietnam. The original Choco Pie is made by a Korean company [Orion Confectionery], but our company produces the Vietnamese version of it, "Phaner Pie." We have a lot of other products, like soft cakes and pastries, but the majority of our production is choco pies.

We started out as a family operation back in the 1990s. Back then we did everything by hand, no machines, and we had to use a lot of human labor just to produce 100 cases a week. Honestly, at the beginning, the choco pies were really hard and didn't taste all that great, but even so it became really popular in the South. In 2000, my parents invested $2 million in an assembly line that could produce 1000 cases of pies in one shift, or something like 6000 cases in a single day. That meant that we were producing much more than we could sell, so we had to find a way to expand. That's when we started to sell in the North and the Center. As sales increased, we invested in a second production line and last year we added a third. The choco pie has really been the basis of our growth all along.

Growing up, I always knew I would end up going into the family business. Originally, I thought I would work on the science and chemistry of the food, maybe in the research and development department. The process of making choco pies is always evolving; to be successful, you have to have good quality control and work continuously to improve the product. But once you've got a good product, you need to be thinking about the sales and financing. That's why I moved to the strategy department. I started out in quality control, then moved to the research and development department, and now I'm a strategist.

I did my high school in Australia and then my Bachelors at the University of Miami in the States. My majors were Chemistry and Economics. Now I'm planning to get an MBA at one of the top ten American business schools. I'm not sure when I'll go, but I'm already starting to apply this year. If I don't get into one of the schools I want, then I'll wait and apply somewhere else. After all, I'm still really young.

Honestly, going to college is more for the networking than the lectures. Business is all about logic, common sense and the way you analyze things. The rest is terminology that you can learn over time. Anyone can do business.

I don't really have a fixed job description. I share the office with the head of sales and marketing. She updates me on the sales situation, promotions and strategy, and I try to help her by providing information about the company. I answer emails from customers. I work with the production manager on any complaints. I even try to do some export sales and generate more revenue. It's all about my future with the company. I'm supposed to replace people in a couple of years when they retire, or find a good CEO to take their place, so I need to understand the company and all its employees inside out.

Usually, I come to the office at 8 a.m. Everything is here in Tân Bình District: the office, the factory, all the equipment, everything. You can smell the choco pies from kilometers away. I only work four hours at the office, then I go and work outside. Being in management, I really don't really get a chance to rest. These days, at noon, I go to District 1 [central Ho Chi Minh City] to the offices of D2 Capital Partners. They're a firm that's helping us with our export expansion. It's pretty far and inconvenient, but I like the commute because it gives me a feel for the city. The people at D2 Capital are working really hard on this project, so they're always calling me with questions. But it's fun. Well, I'm 25, so it's fun now, but maybe later it won't be fun anymore and I'll need an assistant or secretary to handle stuff like this.

I love my job. If I could change anything about it, it would have to be myself. I want to learn more about how to hire and motivate people, and prioritize tasks. For example, it can take up a day just to figure out how to organize a project, and sometimes I'm too lazy to do that. I just jump into a project, and sometimes not everything gets done. This is one of my weaknesses, but I'm learning. I keep a planner, but I still don't like to do anything that doesn't have an immediate effect. If I do something for too long, I'm like, "Oh my gosh, this is so boring." I have to learn to be more patient with the job.

When I'm hiring people, I prefer to choose people who can speak English and have more exposure to Western ideas. What's hard though, is finding the right balance: you don't want someone who's so Westernized that they don't know anything about Vietnamese society. I think Americans are more practical: when they see the benefits, they work harder. When they're given a challenge and opportunity to grow, they'll do it no matter what. They're very disciplined. Vietnamese are less motivated by money, and more by respect, status, and compliments. And in the West, people accept criticism from their boss. In Vietnam, if an employee feels disrespected, they'll go elsewhere. But things are changing. The new generation of Vietnamese students is more ambitious and motivated; they look ahead more.

My monthly salary is barely enough for me to survive. But I'm also a shareholder so I don't really care: the less money I take in salary, the more money there is to invest in the company. Still, I think with my position of Deputy Director I have the highest salary in the company. I make 30 million đồng a month [$1,500]. I don't really have any expenses because I still live at home with my parents: it's part of Vietnamese culture that we don't move out until we get married. So I can keep whatever money I make for myself. But even so, 30 million isn't enough if you live in the city and go out a lot.

I used to read a lot of business books and they're just filled with lots of general cases that all resemble each other. In the real world, even simple problems involve complex issues of personality, family and generations; you can't just look to the case studies in the textbooks for your solution. The best part of my job is the way this company gives me so many opportunities to learn and grow:

it's really far more interesting than all the case studies in all the books I've ever read.

Ho Chi Minh City, October 2010
Thu Nguyen, Nancy Pham, Đào Tuấn Dũng, Nguyễn Hồng Ngân

wedding planner

Although I've already planned so many weddings, it's only now that I'm starting to think about my own [*laughs*]. Being a wedding planner is quite stressful; it's a happy day for the people getting married, but a busy day for us. I can't wait for it to be my day to simply experience the happiness and not be stressed about the details!

My name is Hải. I'm turning 25 this year. I'm in charge of event planning and organizing, mainly weddings, at VCCI Expo [an exhibition center belonging to Vietnam Chamber of Commerce and Industry]. The way I chose this job was pretty random. When people ask, I usually tell them, "I didn't find it, it found me." But thanks to this job, I get to have parties every day without paying a single cent [*laughs*].

Anyway, if you want to have some idea of the kinds of pressure I face as a wedding planner, you're going to have to understand all the tasks I'm in charge of everyday. These days I manage a staff of 120 from various departments. I arrive at the office at 8 a.m., and the first thing I do is check the work schedule on the

notice board. Then at 8:30 a.m., I have a meeting with all the personnel to divide up everything that needs to be done that day. At the end of the meeting, I go back to my office and make a list of my own tasks. At 10 a.m., I visit the wedding location to see how preparations are proceeding. This includes contacting the caterers and checking the list of all the equipment we need for the ceremony. By around 10:30 a.m., the staff begins arranging the tables and chairs, and decorating the entrance gates and the main stage. Then I have to run around a lot to check up on their progress and remind people of any special details.

As you can see, even in the morning it's already stressful in my line of work. But then again, there are some days that are worse than others. It really depends on how many weddings we're setting up that day. On average, I'm usually in charge of managing two weddings per day. But during the peak season, we may have to organize as many as six weddings in one day. And if it's a "lucky" year, the demand can be even higher because people believe holding weddings in those years will bring them good fortune.

The wedding industry is very profitable. Let me break it down for you: right now we have three large banquet halls where we can hold weddings simultaneously. The cost of renting a banquet hall is anywhere between 15 and 25 million đồng [$750–$1250], depending on the time of the year and how hard the couple bargains. Then, each couple will order 100 food trays on average, but we can serve up to a maximum of 600 food trays per hall. The cost of a tray for ten people ranges from 1.2 to 1.5 million đồng [$60–$75]. Of course, the price will be higher if the customers have any special requests. Because each wedding takes place in a relatively short time, only about 1 to 2 hours, there aren't many expensive add-on activities for each wedding besides the food and music. The customers can request to hire singers or if they want to sing themselves, we'll prepare a band or MC for them. The truth is, we make a pretty serious profit from each wedding.

To be able to do this job well, it's really important to be good at improvising. You have to deal with a whole range of situations as quickly and effectively as possible. If you don't, you can have real problems. I remember one time when one of our employees beat up the stage supervisor for something he'd done. You see, with all the work they have to do and the short amount of time they've got to do it in, people can get frustrated easily. If you don't know how to deal with people and their craziness, you won't be able to get anything done. Aside from the ability to deal with crazy people, my other key skills are organizing, planning, and delegating. It's still hard to get training in these sorts of skills in Vietnam, so I had to gain them through my own experience.

Have there been any big changes since I started working as a wedding planner? The only one I can think of is the banning of firecrackers. It's kinda funny, because people immediately adapted by switching to popping balloons on stage. I guess they figured it would create the same air of excitement. When we first started doing it, it was pretty basic: we'd just have two kids holding sticks with nails attached to them and they'd poke each balloon individually to make them pop. Now though, we're very high tech: we just pull a string and all the balloons pass over nails attached to the stage. Boom boom boom boom boom [*laughs*]!

I remember this one time when three weddings were being held at the same time. The problem is that the walls between the banquet halls aren't very well soundproofed. Normally, the start times of the weddings are slightly different. But that day, all three started at the same time and all three had similar scripts. So you had Western music playing on one side, old Vietnamese music on another and karaoke on the other, all at the same time. And when the brides were about to be introduced, we could hear from all three halls, "Please give a big round of applause to welcome the most beautiful woman of the day." All of us staff standing outside couldn't stop laughing [*laughs*].

I've planned weddings for a lot of my close friends. Those weddings are my favorite because even though there's still stress, it feels more rewarding [*smiles*]. But you know, to be honest, after having planned so many weddings here in the big city, I still prefer weddings in the countryside. Even though the planning isn't as professional and maybe the food isn't as hygienic, the atmosphere there is always more genuine and full of excitement. Here in Hanoi, people come in quickly and leave quickly. But honestly, that's just my opinion. At the end of the day, if the couple is happy, we're happy too.

Relations among all the employees at my company are pretty good; everybody helps each other out a lot. But honestly our boss doesn't care much about his employees. There are too few policies to give employees any incentive to work hard, so most staff members don't feel very motivated. I only plan to work here for a short period of time and then I'll start my own business. But for better or worse, I'll never forget the time that I've worked here. It's always a pleasure working with my colleagues to create happy memories for so many people!

Hanoi, November 2011
Nguyễn Thùy Trang, Lena Tran, Maya Weir, Vũ Thu Hiền

multilevel marketer

My name is Linh and I'm a 21 year-old senior at the Foreign Trade University. I'm also a manager at Oriflame's Viking office. This office was founded in November 2009 by a leader who's one year older than me, myself, and some other friends. That was four months after I joined Oriflame. At the time, I already had a network that generated 100 million đồng in monthly profit [$5,000]. I'd known about Oriflame since high school but it was only in 2009 that I officially joined this business. It all started when I was introduced by one of my classmates. After he'd started working for Oriflame, he changed completely from a shy guy to a dynamic, confident, and independent person. Not to mention the fact that he started earning a lot of money! So I got interested and decided to give it a shot.

It's pretty easy to join Oriflame: you must be over 18, submit a copy of your ID card, pay a 89,000 đồng [$4.50] registration fee, and show that you're not currently a member of any other Oriflame branch. The job doesn't have a fixed working schedule, all you need is to be able to set aside around three hours each day. For example, if you were in my group, I could arrange my schedule to meet you at 6 p.m. every Thursday to share our experiences. That's how someone like me is able to work around their studies.

Because Oriflame is a multilevel business, the best way to make money is to recruit and train new salespeople. As a manager, I'm responsible for both direct selling and recruitment, but of course, with a network of 100 people, I've got a lot of responsibility. Obviously, there's no way I can work with all 100 of them personally; my job is to guide and train group leaders, then they'll train their group's members.

You've got to be enthusiastic to do this job; you can't just show customers the catalog and expect to make a sale. You need to know the right bait to hook the customer [*laughs*]. For example, let's say an overweight woman comes to you, and she doesn't know how to lose weight, so you introduce her to Oriflame products designed to help get rid of fat in the hip and thigh area. But what I've realized is that personal experience is the best tool for persuading customers. That's why I use Oriflame products myself.

A great thing about this job is the way it allows me to connect with so many different people. The Viking office recruits 20 new members every day; most of them are students — young, active, and with a lot of spare time. So after two years in this business, I've made thousands of new friendships [*laughs*]. It also strengthens my relationships with old friends or relatives who I might not see so often otherwise. For example, if you work in an office, I could ask you to promote my products in your office; or at home, I'll get my mom to advertise to the neighbors for me [*laughs*].

Of course there are difficulties, like when sales go down in the summer because people use less cosmetics, and my regular customers — mostly my friends — go back to their hometowns. Even though there's no pressure from Oriflame to maintain a certain level of sales, psychologically, it's still tough. And then there's theft. One time my friend wasn't careful when she was watching a bag of cosmetics for me and it was stolen. Or there was the time when I brought an order worth more than 1 million đồng [$50] to school, went to the canteen to chat with my friends, and then I ... forgot about it [*laughs*].

As you probably know, multilevel marketing is often misunderstood in Vietnam because there are a bunch of fraudulent companies who use the term. So I have to be careful when I'm talking about my work. Some people have even asked me right to my face, "It's a scam, isn't it? Why do you work there?" I don't let it get to me [*laughs*]. I know Oriflame is an internationally respected company. Before I decided to join, I'd already done my own research. Now any time people have the wrong idea, I can help them understand better.

I'm really satisfied with my job. For me, as a student from the countryside who has to pay for rent, tuition, utilities, and all the other expenses of daily life, this job not only gives me financial independence but also allows me to put money aside for the future. More important, I've matured a lot working for Oriflame, and gained knowledge and experience I can't get through school. To tell you the truth, I've already had recruiters offer me jobs when they found out that I'm a vice-manager of the Viking office. But wherever my career ends up taking me, I'll stick with Oriflame. This job is like building a house: every day you add a brick and after one year you've got a house. Viking is the house I'm building, and if I build it carefully, it's going to be an asset for me for the rest of my life.

Hanoi, October 2011
Đinh Đoàn Vũ, Nguyễn Thanh Nga, Tracy Nguyen, Trương Công Tuấn

street-side shoe seller

I've always thought of myself as a dynamic person. My name is Trung, and I'm 23 years old. I'm originally from Hải Phòng. My twin brother and I both just graduated from the Foreign Trade University. It's funny, but even though we're twins, we couldn't be more different. He majored in Economics while I studied Business Administration. Now he's working in an office in the

Keangnam building [Keangnam Hanoi Landmark Tower, the tallest skyscraper in Vietnam], while here I am selling shoes on the street [*laughs*].

First off, I want to say that my parents know I sell shoes. In fact, they're the ones who gave me the money to get started. This makes me happy because even though they didn't think it was a good idea, they were still really supportive. In college, I never really tried other things besides studying, so I figure this is my chance to discover where my talents really lie. I told my parents that I wanted to do something "real," to build something I could call my own.

While I was in college, my parents encouraged me to spend all my time learning English. They thought there was no need to spend time doing other things, only studying. I took their advice and ended up spending three years learning English. At the end of it, I realized my English was still pretty mediocre even after I'd put so much effort into it. Then one of my professors told me that English wasn't all that important, and that having skills and creativity was more important. So during my senior year in college, I decided to work harder in my Business classes. At the same time, I also started reading widely. One of the books I really enjoyed was *Rich Dad Poor Dad*. It taught me a lot, but the main thing I took from it was that if you have a good idea, you can make money. It inspired me to start my own business. The only thing was, I didn't know what business to start.

In the end, I got together with a friend of mine and we decided to set up a shop in Phùng Khoang Market. We had to choose between selling clothes, shoes, or something else. Most of the shops in the market sell clothes, so we figured selling something different would be ingenious. That's why we chose shoes. At first we thought we'd made the right decision, but after a while we realized we were wrong. Sure, we're unique because we're the only shop selling shoes, but that's not always a good thing. People come here to buy clothes because there're a lot of clothes shops. When people want shoes, they go somewhere else where there're a lot of shoe shops. People want to have choices, they don't want to be forced to buy from one shop.

These days, I've got a pretty regular schedule. I wake up at around 8 a.m., have some breakfast and then surf the Internet. Some days, I make lunch. After lunch, I play my piano or guitar for half an hour, then I have a nap. At 3 p.m., I wake up and surf the Internet again until 5 p.m. or so, then I start to get ready for work. I'll have dinner before I go, and I'm at the market by 6:30 p.m. We close the shop at 10:30 p.m. When we have enough employees, one of us will stay at the market, while two of us set up our stall on the street here. It takes two people to drive all the shoes out here on two motorbikes.

The worst part of selling shoes on the street is the trouble when it rains. Usually the heavy rain only lasts a few minutes, but we still kill ourselves trying to protect the shoes. We rent some space at a warehouse where we can store the shoes until the rain stops and the sidewalk is dry again. Then there's the police. All of us vendors look out for each other and warn each other if the cops are in the area. Luckily, I've never been caught.

These days, we also sell clothes at the shop in the market. Compared to shoes, selling clothes has a lot of advantages. They're a lot lighter and only come in a few sizes. Let's see if I can think of any advantages to selling shoes. The profit margin is no better: I only add 20,000 to 50,000 đồng [$1.00–$2.50] to the wholesale price, so really, I'm barely making any profit ... nope, can't do it. There really aren't any advantages, only disadvantages.

I'm the first to admit that we never should have started selling shoes. Clothes are way better. But on the bright side, this was an important learning experience for me. It was my mistake to make.

And honestly, I was never in it for the money, only the experience. For example, I've already learned something important: people get their paychecks at the end of the month, so that's when customers are ready to buy. And it's not just the adults: the kids get money from their parents then too. I should probably raise the prices near the end of the month, but I don't. And don't tell anyone, but the price in the market is always going to be higher than here on the street [*laughs*].

I'm looking to the future. I don't plan to be selling shoes three months from now. I'm looking for different options online and elsewhere. All I know is that I don't want to be an employee like my brother. I used to work for a company and it just didn't suit me. I don't want to invest myself in someone else's company, I want to be my own boss and reap all the benefits of my talents and experience. Okay, I know I'll probably have to work for a company for a while. That's how I'll develop my interpersonal and management skills. But I also know someday I'll start my own successful company. After all, I'm a dynamic guy [*laughs*]!

Hanoi, November 2011
Chieu-An Ton Nu, Lê Phương Linh, Peter Lê, Đỗ Đăng Tiến

chapter 8

INVESTING

bank employee

My name is Hiền, and I work for the Sumitomo Mitsui Banking
Corporation in Hanoi. Back when I was a student, I never thought
I'd end up working in a bank. I graduated from the Foreign Trade
University with a degree in International Economics. I always
dreamed of being able to work or teach in a field related to my
major, and having the opportunity to travel a lot. My aunt works
for Citibank, and after I graduated, she encouraged me to apply
for this job with Sumitomo. To tell you the truth, I had absolutely
no experience in banking. But I guess they were impressed with
the way I interviewed, because they arranged for me to do a three
month internship. I've been a regular employee for a year now, and
I've gained a lot of valuable experience in this time.

We're a wholesale bank; that means we don't serve individuals,
only corporations. There's never a queue of customers and we
only do 10 or 12 transactions a day. Normally, I open accounts
and work as a teller; sometimes I do transfers. Everything I do is
systematized. I take a number and input it to the system. Then

I send it to my boss so she can check if there are any mistakes. If there aren't any mistakes, then she'll make the official transaction. Actually my day is quite boring — it's just the same thing over and over again, five days a week, month in and month out.

Japanese people are very strict about everything they do, and Japanese banks have a very serious style. There was one time someone in our office sent a report to the wrong customer by mistake. The director of the bank had to go to both companies in person to apologize. Ever since, only high-level employees are allowed to send reports out of the office, and even then they still have to get approval each time. Or sometimes when you're making a transaction, you may pay a little more or a little less than the actual amount. But even if it's as little as 1,000 đồng [$0.05], our deputy manager will still call the customer to apologize.

My life changed a lot when I started working at the bank. I live with some relatives here in Hanoi, and when I was a student we had a really good relationship. But now I have to work at my office from seven in the morning until seven at night, so I don't have time to help out around the house. My relatives aren't happy with that, and to tell you the truth, neither am I. Your style changes too. Back when I was a student I could dress any way I wanted. But now I have to wear a uniform and can't paint my nails as I like.

There are some perks with this job. I actually just got back from a training course in Singapore and Thailand. The course itself wasn't very interesting: the trainer just talked a lot and seemed to forget about the people he was supposed to be training. The interesting thing was the opportunity to travel to another country, experience a different culture, stay in a four-star hotel, and meet guys. And next month, we're all going to Đà Nẵng on a company vacation. I've never been there before, so I'm really excited.

They try really hard to keep us. Last month they organized a bowling tournament. They divided the employees into ten teams and we competed against each other. It was only my second time bowling. One of our CEOs dressed up as a Vietnamese girl in an áo dài. He made up his face and wore this blue wig. It was really cool.

I really want to find another job that will allow me to be more creative, but it's not easy to quit. For one, I've become really good friends with a lot of my colleagues. We eat lunch together, hang out after work, go shopping... I really like them, and I'll miss them a lot if I ever left. Plus, my boss wants to give me a promotion. I'm already making about $400 a month, and my family likes the idea of me working in a bank. So even though I may think of leaving, I still end up staying.

Honestly, this job is just a stable way to make a living. No one wants to work at a bank because they love banking, they do it because the salary is high and the working conditions are good, or because their families pressure them into it. Basically, I just create and manage a lot of documents. I have no interest in them. My boss is okay, and the interactions with customers can sometimes be interesting, but the Japanese way of organization just confuses me. Sometimes, I think I've already forgotten my original dream.

I feel tired sometimes. On Saturday and Sunday mornings, I wake up and feel so happy that I don't have to go to work. Some of the other girls in my office complain that we're going to be single for the rest of our lives because all we do is work. We don't have any time for a boyfriend, and by the time we get home from work and finish making dinner, we're exhausted. I always tell friends who are still in school to treasure their student days, because they're the happiest and most carefree times you'll ever know.

Hanoi, October 2010
Nguyễn Hương Lan, Son Chau, Micaela Bacon, Lena Tran, Nguyễn Phương Vân

pawnshop owner

I'm Sửu. I was born in 1948 and opened this store in 2003. Before I opened the pawnshop, I owned an auto parts store. But when the road expanded, I lost my house and my store. I can't sell car parts here in my new house because there's not enough space.

I run this pawnshop by myself; my kids have other jobs. My grandson helps me move the motorbikes in and out of the store, though. I chose to do this job because I'm old now and it allows me to just sit here and wait for people who want to pawn their stuff. If I didn't have a pawnshop, I wouldn't have any other job; I'd just stay home and live off my kids [laughs].

To open a pawnshop, you have to get a permit from the district. Then I had to sign an agreement with the police because they're worried about thieves and robbers at night. They also want to make sure I'm not pawning stolen property. There are supposed to be monthly inspections by the police to see if I've got any stolen motorbikes in the shop. They check all my records and receipts. In all, there's the inspection by the ward police, the district police, and the city police. So I guess there are actually three inspections per month.

I open at seven in the morning and work until eight at night. I never stay open past 8 p.m. or the police might fine me. Actually, by law, pawnshops can stay open until nine or ten at night but because I'm old the cops only want me working until eight.

What do people pawn? On average, I get one, two, or even three motorbikes coming in per day, yeah, at most three per day. Cellphones, about two or three a day. Hardly anyone brings in a laptop. The transaction happens pretty quickly — with the amount of time I've spent talking to you just now, I could have already finished a transaction. There isn't really a specific time when customers come in, people can just walk in whenever. Sometimes I'll go two or three days without a customer. When no one comes in, I just sit around. Other times I take a walk and go talk to my neighbors. I don't have to do any housework during business hours: I just sit and watch the shop. My grandson does the cooking and moves the motorbikes in and out.

To figure out how much something's worth, I look at the model and the date of purchase. For example, if you bring in a Wave motorbike that was registered in 2007, it's going to be different than one registered in 2010. If it's from 2010, I'll lend you 10 million [$500]. If it's a model from 2007 or 2008, then I'd do it for 6 or 7 million [$300–350]. And if you don't like the offer, then fine, you can go somewhere else.

Basically, if a bike is worth 10 million [$500], I'll lend you 8 million [$400]. That way, if you don't come back and I have to sell it, then at least I can make some profit. And if you do come back and get the bike, then you owe me interest of course. On 10 million đồng [$500], the interest is 20,000 [$1] a day. On average, I make about 200,000 to 250,000 đồng [$10–12.50] per day from interest; add it up and that's 6 or 7 million đồng [$300–350] per month.

If the owner doesn't come back within ten days, then I have the right to transfer the ownership from them to me. If the customer comes back within ten days and pays the interest, I'll give them an extension for another ten days. Sometimes I make a loss: someone might pawn something for 5 million [$250] but in the end I can only sell it for 4 or 4.5 million [$200–225]. Other times I can make some real money: like this one time when I lent the guy 5 million [$250], got interest, and then still resold the item for 6 million. But I'll never forget the time I lost 4 million đồng [$200]. If it's a regular customer, see, I'll wait longer before selling the item off. So anyway, I lent a guy 20 million [$1,000] for a Honda SCR. Then I waited two months for him to come back but he never did, and while I waited the bike just sat there depreciating. In the end, all I could do was sell it for 16 million [$800] [*laughs*].

Here, only the person who pawns the item can redeem it. It has to be the exactly the same name: it can't just be a relative or something. I keep copies of my customers' ID cards, their driver's licenses, vehicle registration, and the receipt for the loan, of course. No pawnbroker will lend money to someone who brings in collateral but no ID papers. If they don't have their ID with them, then you can be pretty sure that whatever they've got is stolen. Sometimes, though, people have fake papers. How am I supposed to know? I can't tell just by the way they behave!

Most of my regulars are vendors. For example, sellers on Triều Khúc street. They pawn something to me in the morning and I lend them money so that they can go to the wholesale market. Then they sell their goods during the day and in the evening they come and pay me back. It's actually pretty normal for a customer to pawn something in the morning and come back in the afternoon. Unless they're really broke, most customers come back and get their items.

Customers who buy stuff that people don't redeem are usually those who just walk by the shop. Most of them don't have much money. And just like when I take something in, I have to make a copy of my own ID card and the bike's registration when I sell it.

The other pawnbrokers and I don't compete for business. We have a really good relationship; in fact we're all very close. Nobody is going to try to steal anyone else's customers. And if a customer doesn't like my shop, they're welcome to go to one of the others. That said, I'm always happy to have customers in the shop. Heck, I even welcomed you into my shop. But if it's one of those salespeople, I shoo them away. If they talk back to me, I'll smack 'em [*laughs*]. I'm not scared of the customers. Shit! I don't even care if they're police: if they give me lip, I'll still hit them [*laughs*].

Hanoi, November 2011
Annelisa Luong, Nguyễn Thị Lan, Tina Bao-Ngan Ngo, Bùi Hà Phương

bookie

I started working as a bookie when I finished high school. It's already been four years now. My parents are in the same line of work. I guess the reason I chose this profession is because you can't do much in today's society without a degree. Plus I'm used to living an easy life, so I just don't want to do anything involving manual labor.

My work is pretty simple. I take care of clients at different sidewalk cafés. Betting is based on the results of the government lottery. Every day at around 7 p.m., my employees go around to the cafés, collect the money that clients have bet on, and get a record of which clients have bet on which numbers. Then, when the results come out and it turns out a client has won, I figure out the total and give it back to the sidewalk café to give to the client. If the client is still at the café, they can collect the money straightaway as soon as the results come out. In that case, I pay the café owner back the next day. I've been working with all these café owners for a long time, so I don't have to worry that they're going to take the money or give the clients the incorrect amount.

The risk in this business isn't high. For example, if we're

betting "cân bằng," the board has 27 numbers out of 100 that
can win. So for instance, imagine if I had 100 clients who each
bet $50 on a different number. For the clients, as long as all 27
winning numbers have 27 people who bet on them, they can win
around $80 each. But for the bookie, if people have bet on all 100
numbers, then I've already made a few hundred dollars. As long as
100 numbers are bet on, then there's no doubt I've made a profit.

My operation is pretty small-time: there are a lot of bigger
bosses above me. Clients who bet at the cafés tend to bet small
amounts, around a few hundred dollars at most. If the clients are
people we know, and we can be sure they have some assets and
a good reputation, then I can cover bets of up to a few thousand
dollars. All they have to do is call me directly: there's no need for
them to go to a café. As the bet gets bigger though, we may have
to call the big bosses. It depends on the resources we have and
whether or not we're capable of covering the "ôm" [literally "hold,"
i.e., the ability to repay the client if they win].

Here in Hải Phòng, people bet with money rather than points
like they do in Hanoi. And the games are different in the two cities
too. There are different ways you can win and lose, and the payout
changes as well. For instance, if you bet one point in Hanoi, then
you will win about $4. I also place soccer bets. For every bet, I just
cut the price of the bet a little. For instance, if a client bets $5 and
wins, I give them back their bet plus a little over $4. It depends
on each game, though. Most people bet on the European leagues
or the World Cup because in Vietnam all we have to bet on are the
Southeast Asian Games and the Tiger Cup. I've even got my own
betting web page. My page is pretty small — it's only worth about
$50,000 — but I've seen pages that are worth $5 million.

Every profession has its own difficulties. A lot of times clients
lose money and ask for an extension in repaying their debt, so the
circulation of money slows down and this makes life harder for us.

Normally, if a client's got a lot of debt and they can't pay, it's the café owner's responsibility to collect it. It's only when it gets really difficult that I have to collect it myself.

Sometimes the cafés have problems with the police, but this is just so they can make a little money of their own. If someone gets arrested, we have to deal with it. We just give café owners a few hundred dollars for the cops and the situation is solved.

This is my permanent job. Right now, it's simple to sit here and distribute phế [literally "waste"]. It's enough to survive. But the truth is, many of the people I'm close to don't want me doing this for a living. My girlfriend and I have argued about it, but in the end she just has to accept the fact that I've decided to make this my career. Even my parents don't support my decision. But no matter how other people see me, at the end of the day I'm still making a very good living at this. Everyone has a job to do in their life, everyone is different. The important thing is to survive and make a decent living for yourself.

Hải Phòng, September 2010
Tina Ngo, Đoàn Hồng Hải, Peter Del Moral, Nguyễn Hải Yến

lottery ticket seller

My name is Huyền. I'm 21 years old, and I'm a third-year student in the National Economics University. I come from a farming family. In 2005, my family's fields, along with the land of many other families in my village, were appropriated for one of the city's infrastructure projects. Because of that we could no longer make our living by farming. So in order to find a source of income, my family opened this small drinks shop where customers can also bet on the lottery. Anytime I'm not at school, I'm here helping my parents with the shop. I do this both to help the family out and to make a little spending money for myself each month.

I start my day at six in the morning, and prepare everything that we'll need in the shop for the day, like boiling the water, making the tea, getting the ice, cleaning the shop, whatever. I can take people's bets on the lottery any time we're open, but the busiest time is from five to seven in the afternoon. Things start to wind down after that. 7 p.m. — that's when I do the accounting and calculate the amount of money my family earned for the day. My family's lottery business actually belongs to another boss, so as far as income goes, we just make a small commission on the total amount of money we take in.

7:30 p.m. is when the lottery results come out and I can compare people's bets with the day's winning numbers. Then I figure out who won and how much they won so I'm ready when they come to collect the money. Next, I subtract the winnings from the total take so I can settle the bill with the boss. Last, I write all the day's details in our records book so that we've always got an accurate accounting of each day in case we need it later. Sometimes the income from betting is higher than the income from selling drinks, but really, they both depend on the number of customers we get in a day, so our income is very unpredictable.

This kind of work might sound easy, but it's also got its challenges. Customers come in all shapes and sizes: there are kind ones and difficult ones, addicts and hustlers too. A lot of time we get working girls coming into the café, ordering one or maybe two drinks, but bringing with them a whole crowd of six or seven people who take over the place and just sit there for hours. No other customer is going to want to come in when they see that. Or

other times we get young toughs coming in. They tell a few stories and then, before you know it, they're ready to go at each other. It can be really dangerous!

As for betting on the lottery, it's even more problematic. After all, what we do isn't exactly legal, so we've always got to do things secretly. Even so, you're always afraid of an inspection or of being shaken down by the police. And then there're the scammers. Anyone who comes in and makes a bet gets a ticket with the number they bet on and the amount they bet, but there's always someone who tries to alter their ticket or forge a new one when they realize they didn't win.

The way I see it, even without all these problems, it's still a hard job. You've got to be strong and light on your feet if you're going to serve customers efficiently, manage the shop well, and react quickly to whatever happens. Like when there's a fight, you've only got a few seconds to clear away all the breakable stuff so they don't use it to hurt each other. Or if you're not really careful when you're taking a bet, you could lose a lot of money. In the future after I graduate, I want to be an accountant for a foreign company, with a regular monthly salary. I figure that with the way this job has allowed me to perfect my accounting skills and sharpen my sense of judgment, I'm going to have a lot of strengths to offer any company I apply to.

Hanoi, July 2011
Hoàng Huyền Trang

chief operations officer

I was born in November 1980 just a month after my parents
arrived in the US. After they got out of Vietnam in 1979, they
went to Thailand first, then to a refugee camp in the Philippines,
and finally to San Francisco. There are two of us kids; my little
sister was born in 1986. It wasn't easy in the beginning. We lived
in some sort of housing project; I remember a lot of graffiti, bars
on the windows, not being allowed to play outside. My parents
did a lot of different jobs trying to make ends meet. I remember
my dad worked delivering pizza for a while, and if we were lucky
he'd bring a pizza home for us at the end of a shift. My dad had
been some sort of engineer back in Vietnam before 1975, and as
soon as he got to the States he started looking for ways to break
out of the cycle of low-paying jobs. Even while he was working
he was going to school, first vocational college, then community
college, and finally UC Berkeley. He graduated with a degree in
Electrical Engineering and Computer Science in 1986 or '87, and
got a job working for IBM. That really turned our lives around: we
moved to San Jose, bought a house, and basically had a comfortable
middle-class life.

I'd always been in love with the idea of going to Berkeley
like my dad. I remember he used to take me to school with
him sometimes when my mom was working, and it made a
big impression on me. So when I graduated from high school
I was determined to follow in his footsteps and take Electrical
Engineering and Computer Science at Berkeley. But the program
is incredibly competitive, and I didn't have the grades to get in.
Rather than apply to a less competitive major, I decided to apply

for the same program at De Anza community college in the hopes of transferring to Berkeley later. But even for De Anza my grades weren't good enough. That was a big lesson for me. I realized that if something's important to you, you've just got to figure out a way to get it done. So I reapplied to De Anza in Comparative Literature, knowing that no matter what major I declared, I could still take all the same Engineering and Computer classes that I would have taken anyway.

De Anza is one of the best community colleges in California, and I did well there. I guess I thought I was pretty smart, and I let myself pick up some bad habits. Basically I got lazy. So it was a huge shock when I transferred to Berkeley in my third year. Suddenly I went from top of the class with a 3.9 GPA to struggling just to pass. No matter how hard I tried, I kept getting "F"s. It was like the other kids in my classes were speaking a different language. I would look at them and think, "Wow. You are really, really smart." Yeah, I guess you can definitely say I felt a sense of panic. So in my second semester at Berkeley, I dropped all my Computer and Engineering classes and actually started taking Comp Lit classes. I still didn't do well, but at least I survived.

I'd always been into video games when I was a kid. When I was at De Anza I'd had an internship at the company that went on to become RedOctane, and by the time I was at Berkeley the internship had turned into a part-time job. I think I was getting $6 an hour. At the time, the company was kinda like the Netflix of video games: we had this huge selection of games from all over the world that we would rent out to customers. Literally, my job was to go find some obscure Japanese game in our inventory, stuff it in an envelope, and mail it out. For a gamer like me, it was heaven. When I graduated from Berkeley, I asked them for a permanent position. The salary they offered me was seriously low but I took it anyway, partly because I didn't know if I could get a job anywhere else and partly because I really wanted the chance to prove myself. As time went on, the company started producing its own games for niche markets, like a home version of the dance pads you found at arcades. But our first really big hit was Guitar Hero in 2005.

Guitar Hero was one of the first games to bundle the software with a big piece of hardware, namely, a guitar, and then sell the whole package at a premium. At that time, most retail stores were unwilling to carry it, which meant we had to depend almost entirely on direct online sales. The launch was planned for early December, and it was my responsibility to make sure we pulled it off. It was the first time I really stepped up and committed to doing whatever it took to complete a project. I'd never worked so hard in my life. I was doing everything from customer service to hiring extra staff to stuffing the CDs and guitars into the final packaging. But somehow we pulled it off. We sold more than 300,000 units in the first three months, and after a few months we were acquired by Activision. Guitar Hero II went on to sell more than a million units, and Guitar Hero III was the first billion-dollar game in history.

Of course, I'd already left the company by then. First off, some of my co-workers were dicks. Okay, maybe I wasn't the most mature person in the world either, but you can ask anyone who worked for RedOctane back then and they'll know exactly who I'm talking about. But mainly I guess I preferred working at a start-up to working for a big established company like Activision. My dad had worked for a big established company back in the day, too, but that hadn't saved him from being laid off when the tech bubble burst at the end of the 1990s. So rather than entrust my fate to a big company, I preferred to take a gamble on another start-up. At the very least, I'd get to play a key role in doing something new and exciting. And if I was lucky, the gamble would pay off, we'd get acquired, and I could walk away a rich man. Or at least with enough money for a down payment on a house.

I'd gone to Vietnam for the first time back in 2003 on a university exchange program. I'd come to learn more about the country where my parents were from, and while I was there it was hard not to be excited by the energy and potential I saw all around me. While I was still at RedOctane, I'd participated in a Yahoo! forum for Vietnamese Americans, and through that forum I'd been put in touch with a project manager for a major Vietnamese IT company called FPT. He offered me a position on a six month project based in Kuala Lumpur. On the way to KL, I made a brief stop in Hanoi. While I was there, my old professor introduced me to a guy named Landon Schmidt, who was working for a venture capital firm called IDG. They were collaborating with Cyworld, Korea's biggest social network, to create a new online social network for Vietnam. I'd wanted to explore the potential of online communities ever since I'd seen the role word-of-mouth had played in the success of the original Guitar Hero, so this seemed like a perfect match. I started with Cyworld Vietnam in February 2007.

I'm friends with the CEO now, and we laugh about how they low balled me just like RedOctane did. When I started I was only making $700 a month. But I still jumped at the chance; I was that keen to be a part of this project. If I had to point to one difference between myself and our Vietnamese team members, I think it's this willingness to take a risk and make an investment in something. Companies in Vietnam have a huge problem with turnover. Talent in Vietnam doesn't flow to potential; it flows to money and well-known brands. I don't know how many people I've interviewed over the last six years, and not one of them has ever had a question about the company, about our potential for future growth, about the kind of skills and experience they might gain here, no one really cares. These people are pretty good, too: young, smart, talented. But even after they join the company one of my biggest challenges is getting them to stop thinking about the salary alone and start thinking about Cyworld as the outcome of their efforts, as something they're creating for themselves that they can really take pride in.

Maybe it's just a lack of context; the way Vietnam doesn't have the history of entrepreneurship that would help people see the potential in a company like ours. Or maybe it's just that they're being economically rational: after all, nobody has ever let themselves be lowballed like I was [*laughs*]. Don't get me wrong: we have people who have been with the company for years and who've fought hard for us. But they're the exceptions, and a lot of their dedication and hard work is based more on the kinds of relationships we've been able to build rather than any future they see in the company. I still think that generally, people aren't as conscious of building a professional career in the long-run, and that this sort of short-sightedness may have an impact on Vietnam's growth in the long term.

As for me, it's been six years since I joined Cyworld, six years of my life I've invested in this project, and six years that we've been waiting to make it big. It might happen or it might not. But even if it doesn't, I've still played a big role in taking something from a concept to reality. Today, Cyworld is one of Vietnam's largest social networks, with more than 3.5 million users. And I helped make it happen. And in a small way, I've been part of Vietnam's development too, of realizing some of that potential that I saw when I first came back in 2003. No matter what happens in the future, it's already been an incredibly challenging and rewarding six years. I've made some great friends, been able to live and work in both Hanoi and Saigon, and had the chance to get to know and love this place and its people. And I've played a lot of basketball too [*laughs*]. Vietnam has definitely repaid all the investment I've made here. And who knows, even if I never get rich, someday I might still have enough money for that down payment on a house. Not enough for here in Saigon, though, but maybe back in California [*laughs*]!

Saigon, February 2013
Gerard Sasges

chapter 9

PROTECTING

rat catcher

I don't remember when I started doing this. It's just something I've done since childhood, you know, feeding the buffaloes, planting, harvesting, and catching rats in my spare time. It's the way of life that's been handed down to us by our ancestors.

It's a pretty simple job, really, being a rat catcher. The rats show up in October, during the harvest season, in places where the rice has already been harvested. The rats all live in nests in the ground. The nest always has two openings. You just pour water into one hole and wait for them to come out of the other. That's why we have the expression, "wet as a rat's tail." Or you can use the hay that's left over from the harvesting. You burn the hay, use a fan to blow the smoke into one hole, and the rats come running out from the other. Easy!

A lot of folks are afraid of accidentally putting their hand into a snake's nest instead, but actually it's pretty easy to tell a snake's nest from a rat's. Rats are going in and out of their holes all the time, and each time they do, their teeth leave clear marks. In the rainy season, you can see their footprints, too. Some rats are really clever, though: they use hay to camouflage the entrance to their nests. So no matter how careful you are, there are still times when you think you're going to grab a rat but end up holding a snake's head instead.

We cut the tails off all the rats we kill, and bring the tails to the village cooperative. The cooperative collects a fee from all the farmers in the village and sets up a fund for paying us rat catchers. They pay us about 2,000 đồng [10 cents] for each. The more tails you've got, the better [*laughs*]! It's good for both sides, really. The more rats we catch, the less of the rice harvest they eat, and that's good for both the farmer and the cooperative. Once you add in the fact that we can make some extra money from catching a rat, that's three ways to benefit from each dead one.

Last harvest, we got 2,000 đồng for each rat. But this season we'll get around 3,000 đồng [15 cents] each. Obviously, this isn't my full-time job. Even if I catch one or two dozen rats, it's still only 50,000 or 60,000 đồng [$2.50–$3] per day. It's enough to buy some presents for the kids, but if this was my only job, I'd starve [*laughs*]!

We need to kill as many rats as possible; if not they'll breed like crazy. We've got a saying in Vietnamese, "Breeding like rats in October and November." I guess it's easy for the little guys to get in the mood [*laughs*]! That's why everybody's enthusiastic about catching rats: kids, adults, everybody; we're all out in the fields, running around, catching rats. But my god, it never ends! Even if I could catch rats all day every day, there'd still be more to catch.

That's why no matter how many people catch rats, I still don't have to worry about competition. Some people just dig for a day or two, then there're other folks like me who do it throughout the season, during October and November. The rest of the year, though, it's harder. During planting season or when the fields are flooded, the rats can't stay in their nests, and that makes it harder to catch them. Traps aren't very effective, and we don't want to use poison because it might get eaten by the farm animals.

You know, rats are a pretty diverse bunch: there're big ones and small ones, field rats who run fast and city rats who run slow. And you know what else? Field rat meat is delicious — soft and white like chicken. You've probably never seen such things, but there're a lot of ways to prepare them. I remember, at Mrs. Quang's place, I used to watch her chop off the rats' thighs and cook them like frog's legs. Or you can grill the rat whole, or chop it up and make sausages. Delicious [*laughs*]!

These days, though, we usually just use the dead rats for fertilizer. After I cut off the tails, I dig a hole in my field and bury all the bodies. After a while, they decompose and help to fertilize the soil for the next harvest. It's just part of the cycle of farming. Really, this is an occupation that will always be with us. As long as there are people farming the fields, there will be rats. And as long as there are rats, there will be people like me catching them.

Hải Phòng, October 2010
Đào Duy Khương, Đinh Xuân Phương, Vi Le, Katie Do, Emily Shaw

security guard

My name is Minh, I'm 47 years old, and I'm a security guard at the Kim Liên High School in Hanoi. You know, it's funny, but even though I'm not really old enough to be called bác ["older uncle"], for a long time now, the phrase bác bảo vệ ["uncle guard"] has just gotten stuck in people's heads. I guess it's because schools used to hire older men as security guards back in the old days; I guess they'd already retired, but wanted to keep busy by working at the local school. So the image of the elderly security guard has become part of popular culture nowadays. But back then, schools were simple affairs — just four walls and a roof with nothing inside them — so being a security guard was also pretty simple, and those old fellows could still do a good job. But these days things are different you see, so the schools need someone younger who's still got his strength and quick wits.

Basically, my work consists of taking care of the school property, ensuring the security of the school grounds, and ringing the bell to signal the end of each lesson. It doesn't sound too complicated, but it involves a lot of duties you can't really put a name to, like doing rounds to check all the school equipment, making sure the kids remember to turn everything off, directing guests who visit the school, and of course, ringing the bell 32 times a day. It's not about the job description, it's about always being ready to live up to my responsibilities. For example, if I see some kids about to get in a fight, I'll drop whatever I'm doing and come running.

I'd already done more than my share of different jobs before I ended up here. However, I've decided to do this until I retire. I've already worked as a painter, an electrician, a cook, a train conductor; I even set up my own business selling paint. But I've chosen this job because it's easy on my health, and even more important, it lets me spend time with my family. I work shifts, so I can devote my time off to looking after my kids and doing a little work on the side. Even if a job makes you more money, travelling all the time and neglecting your family just isn't worth it.

Working here, I've also got the chance to do some part-time jobs that bring in a little more money during this storm of inflation we're in the middle of. My salary is 2.3 million đồng [$115] a month, but the way prices seem to go up every day, relying on this salary alone is not enough. Luckily, since I've done so many jobs over the years, it's pretty easy for me to find something to do so I can make ends meet. Say, for example, the school needs to refinish the desks, repaint the walls, service the plumbing, or fix the wiring; it's easy enough for me to get the job and make a little extra income.

Choosing your profession is one thing, but the thing that keeps me here is the chance to spend my days in a really cultured environment. Here, I have the chance to interact every day with people of intelligence, people of learning. From the teachers to the students, about 2,000 people in all, each and every one teaches me something, something that makes me a little bit wiser each time I meet them. If I didn't have the chance to talk with the students, how the heck would I know what an iPhone was or how to use it? Compared to working at a train or bus station, places where you can't help but come in contact with criminal elements, the working environment here is safer and more intellectual.

If you feel a connection to something, then you're going to do it with your whole heart. Of course, at the school we've got our share of naughty kids who like to have some fun. But anyone who wants to pass the gates of the school has got to get past me first. That gives me the chance to speak with the little scoundrels. It gives me the chance to speak with them from my heart, to show them how they should behave and how they shouldn't, share some stories from my own experience, make a connection with them. A lot of kids — for example, maybe they have some issues at school — find a way to come have a chat and ask for my advice.

Living with your heart on your sleeve like that, it means I can't begin to count the number of times I've had tears well up in my eyes when I read an essay one of the students wrote about me in class, or in their exams, or in the card they give us on November 20 [Teachers' Day in Vietnam]. Then there are kids who go abroad to study, and as soon as they get back to Vietnam, they come by for a visit, just to show their respect and affection [he quotes the students as using the father-child pronoun pair "bố-con", indicating a particularly close relationship]. These are the sorts of memories no amount of money can ever buy.

Hanoi, July 2011
Nguyễn Thùy Trang

army private

My name is Quang. I'm a private in an artillery regiment stationed at the base in Thạch Thất, Hanoi. I enlisted right after I finished high school in 2011. The army is a bit of a tradition in my family. Both my father and brother are soldiers, but that's not the only reason I enlisted. I also like the kind of person that the military helps me become. It teaches me to be dependable, courageous, and decisive. And it gives me integrity and endurance and the knowledge that I have the loyalty to serve my country if it ever needs me in the future. But it's not easy, that's for sure! There's no turning back once you enlist; you've just got to stick with the program day after day, week after week, month after month.

Let me tell you about an average day in the army. At 5:30 a.m., you're up and out of bed. Fold your blankets, head out to the yard to exercise for 15 minutes, then it's back to the barracks to clean up and have some breakfast. And you'd better make sure you do everything perfectly, because the officers are going to inspect every room to make sure they're clean, each bed is neatly made, and every backpack is packed and ready. We've always got to keep our gear packed because we've got to be ready to go immediately if we get the order to move out.

From 7:15 to 10:30 a.m., we've got a bunch of different classes like military regulations, politics, tactics, and shooting practice. Classes are pretty much the same for all us recruits. We finish morning classes and eat lunch at 10:30 a.m. After lunch, we've got two hours for a nap, then it's back to studying until 4:30 p.m. After classes are over we have an hour and a half to play sports or help with farming, and then get cleaned up again before dinner. We've got free time after dinner, then at 9:30 p.m. it's time for bed so we've got the energy to get up and do it all over again the next day. At the end of each week, the officers announce awards for the best squad and platoon. For fun, we often organize live music shows. We've got some real singing talent in the army, including me [*laughs*]!

So yeah, that's pretty much our week. But let's not forget all the tests. We get tested at the end of each subject, and we'd better do well, or else! Take shooting, for example. During basic training, we go to the range every day and practice with plastic training ammunition. Then at the end of training, we test with real ammunition. They record our results and review our performance for the whole course. If one of the rookies doesn't score well enough, he'll have to be trained all over again, so the instructors

will make him practice overtime until he passes. And if he still can't pass, he's punished. There're different kinds of punishment, like digging holes, helping with farming, or night guard duty. The whole point of being punished is that you have to perform those tasks when other people are sleeping or eating or having free time. It really sucks! And if the initial punishment doesn't work, then the instructors make the whole squad suffer. Everyone in the squad will get punished just because one guy screwed up. It's all part of instilling the idea of "one for all and all for one."

It almost happened to me once. I failed target practice too many times, so they ordered me to dig a hole, a meter round and a meter deep, at noon in the burning sun while all my friends were inside, sleeping. Then I still had to go to class in the afternoon, all sunburned and exhausted and sleepy because I didn't get my nap. But the worst thing was the stress from knowing that if I didn't finish the hole in time, I'd have to dig another one the next day. If I failed again, I'd have two holes to dig on the third day! And if I failed a third time, then my whole squad would be punished with me. And that doesn't mean that they'd help me dig my holes. No, they'd be busy digging their own holes. That meant eight recruits out in the hot sun digging eight individual holes, all because of me. They're not kidding when they call it iron discipline.

But discipline isn't the only challenge we face in the military. When people have to do exactly the same thing day in and day out, they get bored. This can lead to discipline problems, like soldiers neglecting their work or even going AWOL. It's not a problem for me because I knew what to expect; I was already well aware of how military discipline worked. Plus, I was already instilled with the ideals of the Party through my ideological education classes in high school. So even though I get bored sometimes, I have the self-discipline to keep focused on my responsibilities. I'm always aware that I'm serving the country and the people.

Basic training taught me the fundamentals of being a soldier. But it also changed me as a person. I'm more mature and disciplined. You can see it in a lot of different ways, from the way I eat, walk, and wear my clothes to the way I interact with people. If you're not in the military, you can eat and sleep whenever you want, and go wherever you want. Other people may call it "freedom," but I call it "lack of discipline."

Sure, the discipline and the routine can be tough sometimes, but one of the hardest parts of enlisting is leaving your girlfriend or your wife. I remember how I missed my girlfriend like crazy at first, but the officers really helped me to stay focused and prioritize my studies. And with all the letters I wrote and the phone calls I made to my girlfriend, she understood it was my duty and waited until basic training was over and we could see each other again. Which reminds me: to all the rookies' girlfriends or lovers or wives out there, remember that basic training only lasts three months, and your man is only doing his duty to the fatherland. So, sisters, have sympathy for your soldier. Help give them the strength to complete their duty and they'll be home soon.

Hanoi, November 2011
Sean Decker, Phạm Phương Thảo, Huỳnh Đình Quang Minh, Minh Thu Diep

prison inmate

In prison, you have very little control of your life. Everything is hella slow so I have had to learn how to stay calm and patient. I have been incarcerated for 23 years now, ever since I was 18. Since then, I have had many days, weeks, months and years to reflect on my wrong decisions that led me to this life as a prisoner of the state of California. I am a man without a land or home. I have never even had a job in my entire life.

My name is Tuan, and I was born and raised in Phan Thiết. It's in South Vietnam, like a couple hours away from Saigon, now known as Ho Chi Minh City. I was the eighth of 12 kids in my family. After 1978, our parents decided that it was time to get out of Vietnam. By that time, everyone was oppressed and had to live by them Communist rules and laws. It was bad for everyone. We had no reason to stay. Our parents wanted us to have a better life and freedom so we left Vietnam in 1978 from Nha Trang Bay. We escaped by boat with 27 people all together.

Our family was poor and we lived in the ghetto with a bunch of other Asian families. At first, we all got by on welfare. But as the years passed by, we started living the American Dream that we all imagined. Everything here was new to me and life was way more free and exciting compared to life in Vietnam. I was living the good life, but I got caught up partying and using drugs like weed, coke, crystal meth, and heroin. You could say I became the black sheep of my family. I dropped out of high school in the tenth grade, around 1985, I think.

I came to this country as a war refugee when I was a little kid, so I only got a social security number or the green card. I never got legal citizenship or a passport to secure the legality of my position before the law. Because of my committed offenses of felonies, I can be incarcerated as a legal citizen. But since I got incarcerated, the

INS [Immigration and Naturalization Services] has decided to put a hold on me for deportation back to my homeland. So if and when I am up for release from state custody, I am going to be held in Federal INS custody while they wait to do all the paperwork. But Vietnam does not have a deportation treaty with the US. They do not accept my going back!

Lucky for me, I have been trying to educate myself to the best of my ability ever since I've been incarcerated, so that in the future I can join the workforce and become a productive citizen in my community at large. I go to class almost every day: five days a week, if there's no program interruption or lockdown. The class I'm studying for now is a class on Fiber Optic Systems. I am also taking classes for my Telecommunications Certificate that I have to pay for. I'll graduate from this trade in a month or two from now and then I will start working towards studying for my Technician Associates and Customer Service exams. I'm hoping that this education and these vocational trades that I've been learning over the years will help me help my daughter and grandson financially when I get back on the outs. I want to be able to help them and the folks who reached out and helped me while I was locked up.

Tết is coming up, but for me it's just like another day in here and there's nothing so special or so spectacular in bringing in the Tết festival. Maybe the homies and I are going to make a plan to get together and cook something to eat for Tết, but I didn't have any money to go shopping this Christmas to buy rice and Chinese sausages so I could cook them up in a little hotpot, you know? Truth is, I feel a little sad because my little sister forgot to send me the money for me to go to the store and buy some stuff at the Chinese food sale. But it's okay, because I understand that my little sister is very busy with her work and sometimes she is absent-minded and keeps forgetting along the way, you know?

I keep things easy and simple by living my life within my

means. I don't want others to look down on me just because I'm asking for something from them. On the other hand, my family and siblings are having a life of their own on the other side of these fences. They've got their families to care for and their bills to pay. For that, I understand completely. And anyway, it's too late for my little sister to be sending me money to my account now, because my canteen draw has already passed. In prison, you are only allowed to go to the store in the canteen yard once a month, and you have to have the money in your account prior to when your canteen draw comes about. If not, you're not going to shop! And if you miss your canteen draw, you have to be waiting until the next coming month to be able to shop.

I'm very motivated and disciplined, and follow through in all the things that I set my mind to. I'm the type of person who gets it done without any excuses. I do a lot of sit-ups: more than a thousand a day. I find that exercising helps me stay away from all of the drama that happens up in here sometimes. I always walk around the yard by myself and I like to keep it that way. I like to work out in hot and sunny weather, above 90 degrees or 100 degrees. The hotter the weather is, the faster I burn calories when I'm working out on the yard. I don't go to the yard just to hang out and sit around doing nothing. My main purpose is to get out to the yard to work out and stay fit, you feel me?

We get the first Wednesday off every quarterly break here at Corcoran. It's nice to be off since I get to work out all morning period from 9:00 a.m. to 12:00 p.m. Then, I usually play a couple games of basketball with all the homies out on the yard. Here at Corcoran, we play a lot of basketball, almost every day if we don't have class. Especially on the weekends, we play all afternoon. Most of my friends are Asian and we play ball together and kick it. We hang out together and do things together so often, that's how life is behind these walls. Almost everything is racially divided in this institution. I mean, I've got friends across racial lines, but I can't eat, drink, smoke, or have nothing like that with other races; just my own Asian homeboys on the yard and across the penal system. That in itself goes for all races. It really sucks when I think about it, but generally speaking, it's more about politics than anything else, you know what I mean?

I must confess that I am, like the rest of the Asian American community here and at large in the free society, on the high rollercoaster ride of Jeremy Lin, who is also known as "Linsanity" in the basketball world of the NBA. Actually, I'm the biggest, die-hard New York Knicks fan, and not just because of Linsanity who is only now coming into prominence with the Knicks. I have been the biggest fan of the NY Knicks since way back in the early '80s and into the '90s when they were a really, really good basketball team in the East. That is why it was good and great for him to be part of the team and playing a point guard position and all. He's phenomenal — he can pass the ball, has quickness, shoots inside or outside the perimeter, and does three point shots too. And he is also a Harvard graduate. Yeah, Linsanity is the first Asian American who is making all Asians look hella good and proud, not only in America but all around the globe! I even have his picture on my bed wall as my now favorite player of all time with the Knickerbockers. In here, Linsanity has a lot of influence on us all in the Asian community. It really is making us feel proud to be Asian American in this day and age.

This facility used to be capped at 752 inmates but the number has been decreasing ever since the US Supreme Court ruling that capped the entire California prison system at 110,000. Now in facility B, where me and the rest of us are staying, the population of this yard will be cut down to about 452 max, and that's good for us inmates up in here. Less people means less problems and more room for us to manoeuvre between beds. There used to be 16 men sharing one cubicle; now it's been reduced to ten people in one cubicle. They are going to take some beds out from each cubicle in the dorms soon. Yesterday, they moved two guys from my cube to C section; today, they should be moving my next bed neighbor too! Next, they will be taking bed six and seven and moving them out, which leaves me and my bunkie behind at our bunk number five. I'm so happy! I don't have to move out of town, plus there's no one left on my side of the wall, only me and my bunkie.

I have to say life's been good to me lately because I can't really complain about anything. I thank God that I still get to live and breathe fresh air each day; many can't say the same, you know?

California State Prison Corcoran, 2011–2012
Tuan Tran, Annelisa Luong

Note: this interview was taken from letters Tuan wrote to Annelisa between July 2011 and February 2012 as part of the Southeast Asian Prison Outreach Project of the Southeast Asian Student Coalition at UC Berkeley.

chapter 10

REPAIRING
& RECYCLING

knife sharpener

Hi everyone, I'm Thiền. I'm 62 years old, and I'm a knife
sharpener. My main "office" is the corner of a market in Hanoi,
but my hometown is in Xuân Thành, in Nam Định province.
These days I live by myself in Trung Kính. I rent a small room
for 500,000 đồng [$25] a month. The room is small, sure, but it
works for me. My family's still living in my hometown. My old
lady and I have got three children: two daughters and a son. My
daughters are both married and have started their own families.
My son's 21 and he's enlisted in the army.

Overall, my family isn't doing too badly [*laughs*]. We've got
540 square meters of land, and the main house is 50 square meters,
with a flat roof and a modern bathroom [both signs of affluence
in the countryside]. Sometimes, my old lady tells me "You're old
now, and our family's doing fine, why do you need to go so far to
make money? It's not good for your health." I often think about
moving a bit closer to home, but if you want to make a buck,
you've got to accept whatever life throws at you even if it means

being far from your family. As long as you're still healthy, you've got to work. And besides, you become attached to the work. And let's not forget, I make pretty good money. After expenses, I clear about 4 million đồng [$200] a month. With this, I can live comfortably on my own and don't need any help from my kids.

On a typical day, I wake up early, brush my teeth, wash my face, make some tea, and head out at 6:30 a.m. I ride my bike to the market, have breakfast, and begin my day. Depending on how many customers I get in the morning, I can be done as early as 11:30 a.m. or as late as 1 p.m. Then I have lunch and take a break before getting back to work again. Every other afternoon, I switch between Trung Kính Market and Ngã Tư Sở Market. On a slow day, my day can end around five but when it gets busy I can work till as late as seven at night. And when it's slow, I kick back and relax, drink some tea and have a smoke [laughs].

I don't go home very often; I work year-round, so I only go back to my hometown for a few days every couple of weeks or so. I can lose a lot of customers if I'm gone too long. It gets really busy during the three months leading up to Tết. That's when there are a lot of weddings and parties and people need their knives sharpened. Sometimes, it gets so busy I can't always finish my work. Then I go home five days before Tết and stay there for about two weeks before I go back to Hanoi to start the new working year [mở hàng, the first day back at work is considered to set a precedent for the rest of the year]. And then, five days later, I go back home again for the first full moon of the Lunar Year.

People joke around and say things like, "Everyone's got stainless steel knives and their own sharpening tools ... who needs you?" But let me tell you: even if you have stainless steel knives, you still need knife sharpeners like me. Household sharpening tools, electric ones included, are all useless: they just can't compare to my skills. They dull the knives and wear them out much quicker. People who know this value my work.

Even before I was doing this, I had experience sharpening things. I was a carpenter for 30 years, so changing jobs wasn't really a problem. Why did I change jobs? Nowadays, people don't appreciate quality hand-crafted furniture like before; now they just go out and buy some mass-produced junk. So I had to change jobs. At first glance, the work looks easy but it takes a lot of skill and know-how. When I first started, no one trusted me with their knives, so I had to prove myself by sharpening some knives for free. I had to show people I knew what I was doing, and eventually word got around that I was really good. Ever since then, customers came to me [*laughs*]! Now in the blink of an eye, 12 years have passed, and here I am still sharpening knives [*laughs*].

Living in Hanoi, away from my family, can be difficult. Fortunately, I live near some guys from back home; they keep me from getting too homesick. We weren't really friends back in Nam Định, but being far from home brings us together. Or sometimes when I meet other knife sharpeners, I'll drink some tea and smoke some cigarettes with them. We laugh and talk until we just forget about work altogether.

The longer I do this, the more I love my job; I've never thought of quitting. I'll only stop when I'm too old to work, but until then I'll keep sharpening knives. There's no mystery to sharpening knives. Everything's laid out on the table. After all this time, sharpening knives has become second nature to me. It's like playing the guitar. After playing for years, your hands know just where to go and just what to do.

Hanoi, September 2011
Colleen Thuy-Tien Ngo, Mai Lan, Mai Quang Huy, Josh Mayhew

electrical appliance repairman

My name's Trung. I did my undergraduate degree at the Institute
of Science in Saigon; today it's the University of Technology of
Ho Chi Minh City. After I graduated in 1988, I started working
for one of the Army's enterprises where my job was to fix factory
assembly lines. But then my family had some problems. One of my
daughters got a serious brain disease and passed away. Back then,
my salary was so low that I asked to quit so I could use my skills to
repair appliances out of my house. That was January 1991, so it's
been about 20 years already.

The nature of the work has definitely changed. Before, the
economy wasn't very developed and people's incomes weren't very
high, so there weren't many high-tech items to fix. But as the
economy developed, you started to see more color TVs, VCRs, and
video players. Now, there are even more advanced technologies.
But the fact that electronics are becoming more complex isn't a
challenge for me. Actually, even though I mostly fix household
items, I prefer working on electronics. Working on electronics
requires more skill so my rate is higher [laughs]. Nowadays,
I make about 3 million đồng [$150] in one month, or about
100,000 đồng a day. Even though I make more money than I used
to, it's lost a lot of value over the years.

The thing I like the most about this job is the way the
technical skills and knowledge you can acquire are limitless. You
can learn forever and ever. I always feel like I'm swimming in a
huge ocean, like I'm a small person with little knowledge, always
trying to improve myself. But my age makes it hard sometimes.
I know I'll have to quit someday, but I also know I'll regret it
because I love my job. It's not about the money or the status. It's
about one thing: being a person of science and technical skill.

I have so many unforgettable memories that I couldn't tell

them all even if I had all day. But there is one I want to share with you. Now, the start of the summer is when people bring their fans in for repair. There was this very pretty woman that brought in a really dirty fan. I fixed it and cleaned it really well. When she took it home, her husband scolded her for buying a new fan. He said it was a waste, yelled at her and everything. I'd fixed it up so nicely he was sure she'd bought a brand new one! Of course, he had to apologize to her afterward. She told me the story herself [*laughs*].

The only thing I'm not satisfied with is my family's opinion of my job. They just know what they see, but they'll never understand my passion for the job. Because the only person who understands this job is the person doing it. For example, I'll be fixing a TV, and just as I'm about to figure out what's wrong — just like a scientist about to make a discovery — my family calls me to come in and eat lunch. Then I have to stop. In the afternoon, I have to come back and remember where I was. That happens a lot, but I have to empathize with my wife and children because I'm not them. In fact, I guess we all have to empathize with each other [*laughs*]. At the same time, working at home has its advantages: for one, I can take care of the house while I'm working; secondly, I'm always here if my relatives need anything fixed.

I'm 57 years old now and my eyes and hands are getting weak. Before, I could work without wearing my glasses. But now, I have two types of glasses: eyeglasses and my magnifying glass. Before, I could fix things that were smaller. But after I started wearing glasses, within one or two years, I could only work with bigger things. That's why 90 per cent of the things I receive now are common household items. For example, if I have to glue two tiny components together, I have to do it accurately. If my hands start shaking and I glue them together in the wrong position, I'll just make things worse. That's why some repairmen have to retire. In my heart, I want to keep doing this forever, but I know my eyes

and my hands won't let me.

In the 20 years I've been doing this job, what I find most important is this: if you want to hold on to a job for a lifetime, you need to have passion. And to sustain your passion, you need three things: the willingness to ask questions, the desire to continue learning, and the determination not to let yourself get comfortable with what you've already achieved. However, when people first graduate from a school for electronics, the first thing they usually ask is "how much money can you make in one month?" But that's just not something I've ever worried about. For me, what's important is a stable family, a job that suits my life, and a sustained passion for my work.

I have a passion for this job. When I die and reach the other side, I hope that people there will give me things to fix.

Gia Lâm, September 2010
Irene Van, Vũ Hoàng An, Sharon Seegers, Nguyễn Thái Linh

motorbike mechanic

My name is Tú. I'm 32 years old. I came to Hanoi when I was 20 to learn how to fix motorbikes. I studied for three years, not in an official school, but at a small repair shop. That's where I learned the basics. Then after another four years working for other people and gaining experience, I opened my own shop, specializing in fixing and washing motorbikes. I've been my own boss for six years now. I was the first person in my family to do this, but now my little brother also works as a mechanic. Right now, he's helping me manage my other shop on Lê Trọng Tấn Street. I'm married, and we've got one daughter. I rent this house for 10 million đồng [$500]. The shop is on the ground floor and we live upstairs.

To be honest, I failed the college entrance exams. I had no idea what job would allow me to develop a real career. Back then, I thought the best I could do was fix motorbikes. Other jobs like fixing televisions require people to be hard working, diligent, and willing to devote themselves full-time. I didn't want to devote myself to work at that level. It wasn't until I really got involved in this profession that I realized it also requires a lot of skill, technique and devotion.

I open the shop at 7:30 a.m., eat breakfast, and start work if I've got customers. Usually the shop is most crowded from around 8 to 11 a.m. and then from 3 to 6 p.m. If there are no customers, I sit and drink tea or coffee. I work until there are no more customers, which means that there's no designated time for closing the shop. Some days I can end up working until midnight.

My shop repairs all different types of bikes, Vespa, Honda, and Yamaha, whatever. The majority of my customers are university students. While I'm working, I usually give them advice on maintenance, or we talk about different kinds of social issues. Some days, I can have a hundred customers, and other days I only have two, so my income is all over the place. Some days I eat rice, some days I eat porridge [*laughs*]. Right now, we're running a promotion on a basic maintenance package: 75,000 đồng [$3.75] for a manual motorbike and 95,000 [$4.50] for an automatic. I'm running the promotion because it's been slow lately. I can't just sit around playing.

I'm happiest when I can fix a complicated motorbike. However, if it's very difficult, the turnaround time is much longer. I remember how I had to repair a Spacy in 2004. Back then, automatic motorbikes were still rare. We had to take the engine apart, which is something we'd never done before. My crew worked from seven in the morning until eleven the next morning. No sleep. All we ate was instant noodles. But we were finally able to fix it, which made it all worthwhile. When I was still a trainee, I liked to teach myself new things, especially complicated techniques. Now that I own my shop, I still work on difficult cases, but I won't work continuously for 24 hours anymore. I leave it for the next day. I'm no longer motivated to figure everything out at one go.

What are the challenges of this job? It's hard to say. Challenges in what aspects? Finances? Techniques? Or what? I think this job makes a person look filthy. I'm never clean like other people who fix televisions or work in a salon. People in this line of work have to be willing to get dirty. I also inhale a lot of gas fumes, which is bad for my health. And of course, I have demanding customers. It's inevitable with service type jobs; it's the same everywhere you go. In some situations the customer insists we do it their way, so I just do it to get it over with. If anything goes wrong, they're responsible. But sometimes my staff messes up the customers' motorbikes so I have to go about solving the problems. For example, if a customer thinks that we messed up something minor, then we'll listen to them patiently. If it's more serious, then we take it upon ourselves to fix it.

My shop is medium-sized. These days there are a lot of bigger repair shops where people with newer bikes usually go. Bike companies are always introducing new models nowadays. It's like fashion, where you have to follow what's trendy. And motorbikes are becoming more and more complex, so I have to spend a lot of time just keeping up with the new technology. When a case gets too complicated for me to handle, I discuss it with my friends on the phone to see if they've encountered similar situations. That means that it's important to have a wide network of friends in this line of work. My network is a mix of old co-workers, other shop owners and even friends of friends — the more people working together the better!

I pay a fixed salary to my employees. Maybe they've got issues with the amount of money they get, but if they do, they keep it to themselves; I never hear about it. But people have quit on me abruptly, and when I ask around to find out what the issue was, I find out that they had a problem with the money. If I know there's a problem, I try and fix it. I understand that the cost of living is always going up so I have to be flexible with the salary. But on the whole, everybody here seems pretty happy. We like to tease each other and goof around a lot. If we're not happy around each other then we really can't do a good job.

I've got a plan to grow my business by expanding this shop and opening a new branch. However, it all depends on human resources, location and timing. I've also thought about going to study automotive repair, but I decided that I'll probably learn more by working at a shop as opposed to going to a school. I know it won't be as difficult as compared to when I was learning to fix motorbikes because I already have some skills as a mechanic. Plus, now I've got a wide network of colleagues I can learn from. And even though the technology is a lot more modern, I figure I've got enough talent to make learning easier.

Looking back, I think my decision to choose this job when I was young was a good one. I plan on working as a mechanic until I can't do it anymore. But I have to say that even though I still like my job, I don't love it like I did when I was an apprentice. Back then I loved my job, but now I love Uncle more [*laughs*] ["Uncle" refers to former President Hồ Chí Minh, whose image is found on all Vietnamese currency].

Hanoi, November 2011
Hoàng Huyền Trang, Haven Rocha, Ngoc-Diep Tang, Vũ Phương Thảo

recycler

I've been doing this job since 1989, so I guess it's been 20 years already. My home village is in Nam Định, about 100 kilometers from here. It's far from the city, and farming is the main occupation there, so there really isn't much work. That's why I came here to the city, to find work. The first person in my hometown to come work in Hanoi was Mai Quý. When the rest of us saw that she could get work, we gradually started to follow her to the city.

I collect everything: from copper, brass, bronze, aluminum, plastic, iron, steel, and paper, to radios, television sets, and every other kind of electrical appliance. I'm pretty much willing to buy anything as long as someone's willing to sell it. Sometimes, a household might have stuff that could be recycled, but the family doesn't think about it, so I'll come to their door to ask if they have anything they want to sell. If I end up buying a lot of stuff and it gets too heavy for me to carry alone, then I'll rent another motorbike and pay someone to help; it's worth it if it saves me a lot of trips.

After I've bought the stuff and brought it back here, I'll sort and consolidate it so I can sell it on to bigger scrap dealers, who in turn sell it on to even bigger dealers. The scrap dealers here take a lot of different things, but they don't take everything. For example, the aluminum over there, they'll take; the paper over there, they'll take. But all this iron here, I'll have to take up to Thái Nguyên to sell [a province about 75 kilometers from Hanoi, with a number of iron smelters]. Then there're all these computers and electronics. First, I'll take them to resellers to see if they'll buy any of it. Whatever they don't buy, I break down and recycle as plastics and metals along with all the other materials.

In this job, it all depends on your luck. Some days I have so many customers that I'm running around all day, nonstop. But then there are other days where I have no customers at all [*laughs*]. It's kind of like fishing. Sometimes you catch a fish, sometimes you don't. Every day is different.

If someone were to ask me if I liked my job, it'd be hard to reply. I can't really say that I like it, I just do it because there aren't many opportunities back in my hometown. You have to understand, being a farmer is not only hard work — you're out in the fields with the rats and the insects, bent over planting or harvesting, no matter the weather — but the income is also unstable. And whatever I do, it's got to make enough money for my children to go to school. If you subtract all the labor and other costs like fertilizers and pesticides from your profit as a farmer, there isn't much left, even if it's a good harvest. But if you work as a recycler, almost everything is recyclable so you're no longer dependent on the seasons. Plus you've got nothing to lose: you don't have to invest in fertilizers or pesticides, and whatever money you spend to buy stuff, you can get back almost immediately instead of waiting for the harvest.

Of course, everyone would like a nice steady job, but when the only skill you've got is farming, there's really not much else for you to do. I guess I could find a job doing housework or taking care of kids, but it's just not practical. I already have kids of my own so I don't want to be far from them all the time. With this job, I can go home anytime I want to; it gives me a lot of flexibility. And a lot of freedom because no one is telling me what to do [*laughs*]. This job may be difficult, but as long as it gives me enough money to feed my family, I guess I like it [*laughs*].

My two kids are both going to school back in my home village. The oldest is responsible for the rice fields. If there's too much work to be done, he calls me so I can come home to help.

But most of the time, I'm in the city. It's too far to commute, so I've rented a room with some other recyclers near the intersection of Văn Chương and Tôn Đức Thắng. Sometimes I feel guilty for being so far from my family. I've tried to find work in the village, I've looked high and low, but there's just no work for me. And even if I did find a job in the village, the salary wouldn't be enough to support my family. So in the end, I'll just keep doing this job until something better comes along.

Hanoi, November 2010
Kristine Nguyen, Đinh Hà Thu, Mary Luc, Jesse Van Fleet, Nguyễn Phương Chi

chapter 11
CLEANING

domestic helper

My name is Quý, and I'm from Xuân Vinh in Nam Định Province. Everyone calls me Auntie Xuân, after my husband. I moved to Hanoi from the countryside more than 10 years ago; exactly 15 years ago, now that I think about it. When I was still living in the countryside, I did farm work, but the most you could earn was the food on your table. Because we wanted a higher standard of living, my husband and I decided to move to the city.

When we were first living here, I really missed my family and my home. Now, though, I've moved on and gotten used to focusing on my present life in the city. I still visit my home village every once in awhile, but nowadays while I'm there I miss the money I make in the city [*laughs*].

Actually, it was my husband who came to the city first, working driving a cyclo [a cycle-rickshaw with the passenger seated in front] while I stayed home and took care of the farm. Everybody said living in the city would provide him with a lot of opportunities, but you know what happened? People kept stealing his cyclo, his only means of making a living. It happened six times. Each time, he would buy a new cyclo and go back to work, and then it would get stolen again. After I heard how hard it was for my husband, I decided to move to the city to help him. After a year with both of us earning, we were able to buy a motorbike for him to start working as a xe ôm [motorbike taxi] driver.

We really had to think long and hard before making the decision to move to Hanoi. We've got a big family, and we knew that if my husband and I went to the city for work, our three kids would be back in the village alone, taking care of each other and going to school all on their own. At the time, my oldest was only 12 years old; at that age he already had to be responsible for his younger siblings. We were so lucky that our neighbors, my parents, and our brothers and sisters all pitched in to help take care of our kids. It's thanks to them that our children didn't have to face too many hardships while their parents were away.

These days, I work a lot to earn as much money as possible. I may be old, but I'm still healthy. Even though my kids now have stable jobs of their own, and they'd all prefer for me just to stay home and take it easy, I want to work while I still can. They have their own families to take care of. I really want to be self-sufficient as long as possible, and to put aside some money so that I don't have to live off my kids when I'm older and can't work any more.

An ordinary work day starts at 6 a.m., when I catch the bus to Gia Lâm [part of the Hanoi metropolitan area on the east side of the Red River], where I clean the family home of a woman named Mrs. Hạnh. Her children own a large taxi company, so after I finish cleaning their home I clean the company offices. I've been cleaning for them for nearly ten years. In the office, I clean with a broom and a mop, but when I'm cleaning a house, I get down on my hands and knees and clean by hand to make sure the floor is as clean as possible. When I first started working as a cleaner, I used to get pain in my arms, but after awhile I got used to it. I have another job two days a week ironing clothes for a lady named Mrs. Trang, who was introduced to me by Mrs. Hạnh. Interestingly, Trang ended up marrying a Westerner, and now she's got a very comfortable life.

Sometimes I make a little extra money by buying old things and recyclable materials from people. Then I resell whatever I buy to recyclers. I only do this on days when I don't have cleaning or ironing to do. In the evening when I'm finished with the cleaning and ironing, I catch the bus back home and continue working, washing dishes for a nearby restaurant. That takes me another hour or hour and a half, depending on whether I wash quickly or slowly. I get to bed at around 10:30 every night after I've finished all the household chores.

My employers are really nice. Sometimes they offer me food and water; one time, they gave me a fan to take home for the house. Because they're so good to me, I really try hard to be careful when cleaning, to make sure everything is orderly and nothing is out of place. Just the other day, one of my employers even gave me their beautiful big TV when they wanted to switch to an LCD TV. Because we have such an established relationship, whenever I'm at my home in the countryside, they always call me if they ever need me to work. They place a lot of trust in me.

Hanoi's changed so much since I first came here. 15 years ago, the area where I'm renting a room was just a field covered in wild rice. Now, houses and apartments are popping up like mushrooms after the rain. And as people get richer, there's more private property and more demand for my cleaning services.

My income in Hanoi is four to five times higher than what I'd be making if I'd stayed back in the village. Sometimes, people are generous and pay me 400,000 đồng [$20], but usually it's 200,000 [$10] for a day's work from morning to night. In the evening, I make another 45,000 đồng [$2.25] washing dishes. Each month, our room costs us 800,000 [$40], but if you add in electricity and water, it's over 1 million [$50]. Three meals a day costs about 40,000 to 50,000 đồng [$2–$2.50]. I often prepare meals at home: it's a lot cheaper than eating out. I can bring rice from my home in the countryside, but I have to buy the vegetables and meat at the market. In an average month, I can save as much as 2 million đồng [$100].

I work not just so I can afford the cost of living in the city, but also to help support my family at home in the countryside. With the money I make in the city, we can buy a lot of things: school supplies for the grandkids, motorcycles, TVs, and let's not forget paying for the kids' weddings. So whenever I have work, I work hard. Really, I've got nothing to complain about. Sometimes I get a cold or the flu, but just a few Tiffy pills for 5,000 đồng [25 cents] and I'm right as rain. But when I get old and can't work anymore, I'll return to the hometown and my family. What would I do in Hanoi? It's just a big, crowded, sweaty, noisy city.

Hanoi, September 2010
Micaela Bacon, Lena Tran, Nguyễn Hương Lan Nguyễn Phương Vân, Son Chau

shoe shiner

My name is Sơn and my hometown is in Nam Định province. I'm 26 years old. After I finished secondary school back in my hometown, I went to Hanoi to work and I've been working here for ten years already. I work for the national railway company, and when I'm not working there, I shine shoes.

There are three kids in my family; I'm the youngest. My brother and sister live in the countryside. They work in the fields as farmers or they just sell small goods here and there. As for me, I have a wife and a one-year-old daughter. My wife farms in the countryside and I work in Hanoi. I send home any extra money I make to my family. It's not a lot of money because the cost of living here is quite high, but usually I send about 1 million đồng [$50] back a month. It used to be easy to save money. Now, money loses its value so quickly that I just can't save as much anymore. It doesn't matter how hard I try.

During the weekends, I start work at 8 a.m. and keep shining shoes for the whole day. Eight to nine in the morning is when I get the most customers. That's when they're usually sitting at cafés, having their coffee, reading the paper, or just chatting with each other. For my job, I basically just wander around the Old Quarter for the whole day. In the afternoon, I go back to the guest house in Phúc Tân to have some lunch. I rent my own room; I don't share the space with anyone. I take another break for some food from 6 to 6:30 p.m. By seven, the sky is starting to get dark, so I continue wandering around a little longer and then stop. As for my job with the railway, I have to work all day and the pay isn't high either: 2 million đồng [$100] a month. On weekdays, I start at 8 a.m. and finish at 4 p.m. Afterward, I make time to go shine shoes for another two or three hours.

When I see a potential customer, I just invite them to get their shoes shined. In general, rich people want their shoes shined more often. When I shine a pair of shoes, I give the customer these plastic flip-flops to wear while I'm shining. Beside dress shoes, I can also polish athletic shoes with water and soap. I charge 7,000 đồng {30 cents} for each pair of shoes. Normally, I polish shoes for Vietnamese people. If I offer the service to Westerners and they accept, then I'll do it. If they don't want it, then I move on. There are a lot of shoe shiners who beg Westerners, even try to take their shoes off for them, but that's not how I do it; I won't beg. Most of my customers are regular customers. I like regular customers; while I'm shining their shoes we can joke around a little.

The hard part about this job is always having to walk around to find customers. That's when it's easy to get caught by the cops. For several years now, the cops have been cracking down on shoe shiners. And if they catch us, it's not just to fine us: no, they put us in jail. For the first offense, we get 15 days in Đầm Dầu jail in Đông Anh. A second offense means three months at Ba Vì, the third means six months, and so on. In Đầm Dầu jail they didn't make me do much, they just locked me up. But in Ba Vì, they say the inmates have to tend cows and stuff. Luckily, I've only been to Đầm Dầu [laughs].

When I first started shining shoes, we used to carry our polish and brushes around in a special wooden box. But ever since the cops have been cracking down on us, we've had to disguise ourselves. We put our gear in shopping baskets or plastic bags. But at least these days the cops don't chase us like they did a few years ago. Now it's only when they get a special order that they come after us. I don't know why they target shoe shiners. I only know that they get the order from higher-ups. Maybe they think we're homeless people and that we're bad for the city's image.

Hanoi has changed a lot since I started working here ten years ago. The streets used to have more walking space, but these days there're so many cars and motorbikes — it's very cramped. Back in the day, shoe shiners had their own turf, and each one just worked their own area. But that system had already broken down by the time I started working in Hanoi. When I first started, there was a lot of competition, but not anymore. Now, there aren't many shoe shiners left in Hanoi. Us ones that are left, we avoid each other; if I see that there's already a shoe shiner at a café, I won't go in.

In general, I love the sense of freedom this job gives me. I don't like the feeling of being tied down. For example, I wouldn't want to be a security guard because it would force me to sit still all day. But then sometimes I look at people with stable jobs, and then I look at myself, just wandering around aimlessly my whole life. Then, I pity myself.

I have no idea about the future of this job. My friends don't even do it anymore. As for me, for now, I'll just keep on doing what I'm doing. If I could choose another job in the future, I'd want to be a taxi driver because it's easier to earn money. I've got some friends who've become taxi drivers. I'd like to learn to drive, but I can't afford to pay for the lessons. Mainly, though, I have to think about the future of my little girl. I have to find a way to put her through school so she can have a higher level of education compared to what I was able to get. We can't have her end up just wandering around endlessly like her father [*laughs*].

Hanoi, October 2011
Lê Phương Linh, Peter Le, Đỗ Đăng Tiến, Chieu-An Ton Nu

laundromat owner

My name is Thể Trịnh, but I took the name "Sharon" when I arrived in the States. I'm originally from Phan Thiết. My mother and father were both Teochew Chinese, but they escaped China to live in Vietnam. I'm the middle child of the family; I grew up with four brothers and four sisters. In America, I live with my husband, my older sister, and my two daughters when they're not at college. We settled down in San Jose after moving around a lot in the 1980s.

We tried so many things before we started up our laundromat. My husband and I met in Boston, so we initially tried to do nails on the East Coast. It was popular for Vietnamese to do nails because it's easy and requires no English-language skills. It wasn't working out for my husband though, so he ended up delivering pizza. When I was pregnant with my first daughter, I got an injury that limited my ability to do nails. So I stopped working at the nail salon and we moved to LA where my sister and her husband were looking for jobs as well. We did random business stuff. Finally, my husband decided to move to San Jose to work at a computer repair shop with a business partner. That guy cheated us, so we stopped working with him. Then my sisters in Long Beach wanted to try opening a bánh mỳ [Vietnamese sandwich] shop so we moved back down to Long Beach to set it up. After a year, we realized that wasn't working so we moved back to San Jose. By this time, it was 1997. Next, we started a water store called "Pure Water." We did this until 1999 when we sold the water store to my brother-in-law and started up our laundromat.

We finally settled down with this store. It's a 20-minute commute to work every morning by car. There aren't any skills needed to run this store, really. We just run the machines and do laundry drop-offs; it's all about washing, drying, and folding other people's dirty clothes. In terms of how to run the business, we just learned from friends and family.

An ordinary work day starts at 5 a.m. That's when I have to wake up to get ready so I can open the store by 7 a.m. Sometimes, customers like to wash their clothes in the morning before they go to work so I have to be prompt in opening up the store. I usually have a couple loads of drop-offs a day. We weigh the load and then sort the dirty clothes before we wash them. When they're done, I throw them in the dryer; then I fold them and pack them into bags and onto hangers. I like to interact with the regulars and they really like me, so a lot of them are my friends. Sometimes, I give them a free soda or let them use my detergent. Most customers are from nearby neighborhoods. People come and go because the economy is bad. No one sticks around for long. Over the years, fewer and fewer people use laundromats because they buy their own machines for their home. The drop-off clients are usually the wealthier people who can afford to pay $1 per pound for us to do their laundry for them. Around five o'clock, my husband comes to take the night shift. He wipes down all the machines and mops the floor. If there are still drop-offs to do, he'll finish them up for me. He closes up the shop by ten every night. We've tried to work with different friends, but we don't like it because doing business with friends can be bad for the friendship. Mostly, it's been me and my husband. Sometimes, my sister comes to help, but she's busy helping with another family business as well.

Because of the long hours, I don't get to eat my lunch sometimes. There is really no time to rest at the store because I constantly have to manage the machines, the drop-offs, the customers and everything else. Sometimes, my husband will work the whole day so I can go out and buy supplies and materials for the store, like more detergent, laundry bags, or hangers. Since we run our own business, there's practically no vacation time. We only close on Thanksgiving and Christmas day. If I ever want to go on a vacation, my husband will take all my shifts and do extra duty so that I can travel. We never get to go on vacation together because one of us always has to watch over the store. I only go two weeks at a time so he doesn't overwork himself.

Our profit margin is low, so we don't make a lot. Our income fluctuates according to the seasons. In the summer, people do less laundry because they wear less clothes. In the winter, they wear more layers and have to wash them more often. This kind of business depends on the economy too, so if the economy is down, our business goes down as well. I think our business is slowly declining and we can't do anything about it. It will only help us get by, and I hope that I can retire, or at least work less, once my daughters graduate and get their own jobs.

This job is challenging because it's a lot of work. It's not a good job to be washing and folding dirty clothes every day. Sometimes, we have homeless people coming in to sleep in our store. Or there's a robbery. It's happened a couple of times. But the biggest problem is always money. Fewer and fewer people come to the laundromat. So the real challenge in my life is to be at peace. I don't want everything to be about money. I just want to find peace and happiness even though I have to work so many hours a day. This is just the reality of life.

I don't think this profession gets a lot of respect. Why would anybody want to wash other people's clothes? I want my kids to understand this so they can avoid this type of future. They can do anything they want; I always have and always will support them in their future, just as long as it's not the same as mine. I know it's hard, but I want a better future for my kids. I want them to go to school and graduate and find a good job. I don't need them to support me in the future, I just want them to be happy. This is not my dream job, but this is the best I've come up with. It's good sometimes because I get to keep busy and not get bored with my life. The worst part is just always being in debt. But I'll always appreciate the interesting people that have come and gone through this store.

I'm old now but I still want to keep busy because there's nothing else in life I need to do. I'm happy and I keep working because I want my family to be okay. Sure, we'll always have to struggle, but we came all the way to America for this kind of life.

San Jose, July 2011
Tracy Nguyen

chapter 12

GROOMING

barber

My dad was a barber and he passed the profession down to me. I'm 35 years old. My hometown is in Hà Nam province, but I've been living and earning a living in Hanoi for a while now. I just got married recently, which is actually pretty late. My wife works at a state-owned shoe factory; it's a good, stable job to have.

Given that I'm a street-side barber, I guess you could describe my workspace as quite spacious [*laughs*]. Five years ago, there was an HIV-prevention project in Hanoi. As part of the project, they concentrated all the street-side barbers into three different areas around the city. I think this is the only one of the three that's left today. I'm not sure why; maybe it's because the sidewalk here is wide and we don't impact the local businesses. Plus, there just aren't that many places left in Hanoi where you can have 12 barbers all working alongside each other.

Ever since we started working here, we've been working nonstop — even on the first and second day of each lunar month, when people consider it unlucky to get a haircut. Every job has its pressures, including this one. Customers can be difficult, or make special requests. If that happens, I just tell them: "If you're not satisfied this time, you can go to another barber the next time." That's it: if I do a good job, they come back; if not, I'll never see them again.

Most of my customers are men, and most of them are regulars. I get customers of every age, from little kids to old men. Some men get a shave too, but not that many. I like to talk to customers while I'm cutting their hair; some of the older ones with a lot of life experience can be really interesting to talk to.

Hanoians enjoy the convenience and the atmosphere of getting a haircut in the open air. Most of my customers are middle-class; they have the money to go to a salon, but they still come here to get their hair cut on the street. Plus, there's the problem of your wife seeing your new haircut and asking, "Where did you get your hair cut, honey?" You see, there're a lot of salons that specialize in men's haircuts, where they've got a lot of young women employees, and well I wouldn't know myself, but customers tell me the girls can get very touchy-feely, if you know what I mean. A man can avoid a lot of questions if he can tell his wife he got his haircut on the street.

Even though my father passed the profession on to me, I still tried my hand at different jobs before I decided to make cutting hair my career. That's why I only became a barber when I was 25. To tell you the truth, in the beginning I didn't like the job because most people didn't take very good care of their hair and beards back then. But that's changed a lot over the years. Since I first started, I've worked at three different places: two years in my hometown, three years at the Security University in Thanh Xuân District, and five years here. I remember when I first started cutting hair: I actually managed to hurt both the president and vice-president of my commune [*laughs*]. I'll admit, even after ten years, I still make mistakes sometimes.

There's a little competition, but nothing serious; basically, you cut your customers' hair, and I cut mine, that's it. In an average day, I probably do ten haircuts and make about 350,000 đồng [$17.50]. My equipment isn't expensive, less than 2 million đồng [$100] all in. My only real expenses are the fees for electricity, garbage, and renting a little space to store my equipment at the local school every night. When I first started, I used to earn 2 or 3 million đồng [$100 or $150] a month, but with inflation being the way it is, these days I earn around 10 million [$500] a month. Compared to other jobs, that's pretty normal. It's thanks to being a barber that I've already saved enough money to buy some land and build a house in Hanoi.

I'm my own boss, so this job comes with a lot of freedom and flexibility. I start when I want to start and stop when I want to stop. I usually start working around 8 a.m. I'm providing a service, so if a customer comes, I'll cut their hair even if it's lunchtime. But when I leave for my lunchtime break, I close up the shop and leave for half an hour to an hour. My house is 10 kilometers away, which is a little too far for me to travel for my lunchtime nap. I'll just nap in the chair here if I don't have any customers. During summertime, I close up at around 7 p.m., and in the winter maybe 6 p.m. If customers are still coming and I don't have anything else to do, I'll cut their hair, but if I'm busy, they'll just have to come back another day.

I've got some nice memories from this job. I remember one time when a high school on Láng street hired me to give haircuts to their students. Another barber and I worked just half the morning and we made several hundred thousand each; I don't even know how many heads we worked on that morning. Then this other time, this rich businessman hired me to come to his house and give haircuts to him and his two kids. When I got to his house, it was so beautiful and fancy that I thought that he must work for the government for sure. I'm happy to say that I still go to his house once a month to cut his hair.

Cutting hair isn't easy. It's an art, really, and it's difficult to do well. I guess that's one of the reasons I love this job. I've already trained three people to be barbers, and when my son turns 14 or 15, I'll teach him the art of cutting hair too. Why not? It's a decent job. Once I teach my son how to cut hair, no matter what happens, he'll always be able to build his own business. Every job has advantages and disadvantages; but in the end, the important thing is to make an honest living. That's it!

Hanoi, November 2011
Chieu-An Ton Nu, Peter Le, Lê Phương Linh, Đỗ Đăng Tiến

scale lady

At first, when people hear what I do, they think it's a weird job. I'm a scale lady. Actually, the name of my job is exactly what I do. It's simple! Every day I walk all over the city with my scale, and whoever wants to know their weight and height can pay me to measure them.

I'm from Hưng Yên, but I rent a room at Ngã Tư Sở when I'm in Hanoi. I've got three kids; my two daughters are married and have families already and my youngest is in the twelfth grade. Back home, the whole family farms; I'm the only one with a job in Hanoi. The money I make goes to paying my kids' tuition fees, buying fertilizer for the fields and food for the table; I don't have money left for myself. Whenever there's no work on the farm, I go to Hanoi to weigh people. I stay for about ten days at a time, maybe half a month at the most, and then I go back to my village. My husband and son are at home, I still have to go home and take care of them sometimes, don't I [*laughs*]? And going back and forth like this all the time, my husband and I really have to trust each other too [*laughs*].

I usually start working at 8 a.m. and walk from street to street around Bùi Xuân Trạch. Whenever I come across a customer, I weigh them and measure their height. At around 12:30 p.m., I push my scale home, cook lunch, take a nap until 3 p.m. and then go back to work. In the afternoon, I try to pick a spot that has a lot of people walking by. Around 5:30 p.m., I usually set up at the playing field at Hanoi University. Sitting there, some days I get 20 customers, but others I only get ten; it all depends. Then around 7 p.m., I go sit by the phở restaurants on Nguyễn Quý Đức street. I don't know why, but for some reason, people like to get weighed after they eat. I sit there on Nguyễn Quý Đức street until about 10 p.m., then I start walking home. I usually get home about 11 p.m., then I cook dinner and have a shower. I normally go to bed by 12:30 at night. Altogether, I walk approximately 25 kilometers every day. I stay home only when there's a big storm. Sure, it's really tiring, but I've got to make a living.

Before I go to work every morning, I prepare my supplies: some water to drink, my hat for when it's sunny, and of course, my raincoat. In general, I don't have to spend any money when I'm working. Some days I make a lot and some days I make a little. On average I make about 200,000 đồng [$10] a day. Deduct 50,000 [$2.50] for my daily expenses, and I only save 150,000 a day [$7.50]. I cook all my meals myself, that way I only spend about 20,000 to 22,000 đồng [$1.00–$1.10] on food a day. I eat less so I can save more money; if I didn't, what money would I have? But I still try to eat enough to stay healthy for my job.

I've been doing this for 11 years. I was introduced to it by another person in the village. That's how it works: one person in the village starts a new job, then they introduce it to another person, and so on. The people in the village who first started this have been doing it for 20 years already. I bought my scale right in the village; some villagers go to China to buy the scales and bring them back. Mine was already used, but it still cost 4,000,000 đồng [$200]. If I tried to sell it now though, I wouldn't get that much.

After I bought the scale, I came to Hanoi and stayed with my sister-in-law. She'd already been working as a scale lady for a while. She taught me how to use the scale, showed me the ropes. Even so, I worried a lot in that first year. I didn't know if I had the strength to keep it up, worried about not knowing my way around the city. I lost a lot of sleep in my first month here. But I got used to the work after awhile.

You have to be careful. It's easy to get caught by the police if you don't know which street doesn't allow vendors. My sister-in-law got caught once. The cops took her battery and wouldn't give it back, so she had to buy a new one for 800,000 [$40]. I make sure I don't go down streets where street vendors are banned; I don't want any trouble with the cops.

If the scale breaks, I can fix it myself most of the time. But if I can't fix it, I have to bring it back to the village and get someone to repair it. You know, one time my scale broke and I couldn't fix it so I had to push it 38 kilometers, all the way home. If I didn't do that, I'd have had to take a xe ôm [motorbike taxi] and waste 200,000 đồng [$10].

Working at night, you run into a lot of drunks and drug addicts, especially on Nguyễn Quý Đức street, that's where I meet them the most. Sometimes, they won't pay me or they try to mess with my scale after I weigh them. To prevent them from stealing it, I have to lie and tell them it's not my scale and that I simply rent it. Even then, sometimes they still keep messing with it. They've broken it three times. They're assholes. But I've still got to be polite to them. You know, some of these jerks are the same age as my son, but still it's me that's got to be nice and respectful.

In my village, people would come help me if they saw something like that happening. But here in the city, people just stand and watch. In the village, everyone looks out for each other; but people here only look out for themselves. I don't know; maybe it's because they know I'm not from Hanoi, so they figure it's not their responsibility to help me. But still, I can't help feeling sad and sorry for myself whenever it happens. But what can you do? That's life [*sighs*].

Luckily, I've never been mugged. My sister-in-law has been mugged twice by heroin addicts. They threatened her with their syringes if she didn't hand over her money. You see, this is a dangerous job. I only do it because I have to. It's just so hard to make money back in the village.

It's also a sad job. I'm alone all the time, I walk the streets alone, I wait for customers alone. Customers come, pay money, and leave without talking to me. It's a sad job but what else is there to do? The more I do it, the more it becomes a habit, the more I get used to working alone. But there are nice customers, too. It costs 3,000 đồng [15 cents] to get weighed, but these customers pay me more, 5,000 or even 10,000 [25 or 50 cents], and they won't take change. They tell me to use it to buy some water so I don't feel so tired. Whenever that happens, I feel really touched. But then again, there are also customers who try to bargain with me [*sighs*].

I'm good at my job. I'll keep doing it as long as I'm still healthy. And when I no longer have the strength, I'll go back to the village and sell vegetables. My son is going to college this year; I expect a lot from him. My son-in-law has a business fixing electronics, so my son wants to work with him after he finishes college. That's good; as long as he's got a job, then it'll be worth all the walking I've done all these years!

Hanoi, September 2011
Michelle Ta, Ngô Mai Hương, Tina Thy Pham, Nguyễn Hà Phương Ninh

grey hair plucker

Hello, sit down please! Oh, my name? My name is Hằng. How old am I? I was born in '87, so please don't call me chị [older sister], it makes me sound so old [*laughs*]! This is one of the first grey hair plucking shops in Hanoi. It's been open for three years now. I've been working here for about a year after one of my friends introduced me to the job.

I was born in Hanoi, and I started looking for work after I graduated from high school. For a while, I worked part-time as a sales associate in a clothes shop. For that job, I needed to have a high school diploma and good sales skills. But this is the best job I've had by far. I live nearby, so it's super convenient for me. And while I'm here, well, I'm just here. The work is really easy and suitable for girls.

I had to do a week of training before I could become an official staff member. A normal day starts at 9 a.m. and ends at 7 p.m., but the number of customers varies day by day. Most of our customers are office workers and are pretty evenly split between women and men. To work here, you have to be honest, self-disciplined, and

there's definitely no listening to your own music while working. In our store, we only play easy-listening music.

I get along well with my co-workers; we're like brothers and sisters. And the owner is really friendly. He's easygoing, and he lets us choose whether we want to work full-time or part-time. For Tết he even took all of us out to eat together.

One of my favorite things about working here is getting to know the regular customers. They talk a lot while I'm plucking their hair, you know, they share about their family and their lives and stuff. But my boss warned us beforehand, "Don't get too close to the customers," so we're always careful to keep things professional. Actually, some customers really like me; they think of me as a daughter or granddaughter. In the old days, only little kids would pluck their parents' or grandparents' white hair right? So customers tend to see me in that light. Nobody ever looks down on me.

When I first started, my salary was 1.8 million đồng [$90] a month, but after one year I'll get 2 million [$100]. I get a raise every year on the anniversary of the day they opened the shop, and then some bonuses for working extra days. It's enough for me. I live with my family and don't have to pay rent, so I've still got lots to go to the café with my friends. And it's a fair salary, I think. After all, each head takes a different amount of time. For example, say someone comes in and I spend two hours plucking their hair. That works out to 60,000 đồng [$3] an hour. Plus, I never have to work overtime. There was one day when it was time to close the shop but one of the customers only had half of his head plucked. We just asked him to come back the next day to get the rest of his head plucked. Well, he came back, and we took care of it [laughs].

Some of my friends were surprised at first when I told them about the job, but when they come and see what I do, they like it. My parents think my job is pretty okay. After they came to see the store, they gave me permission to work here. This shop is different from other hair shops. We specialize in plucking white hair, and no customers ask for other services [a reference to massage/sexual services available at many hair salons for men]. The customers here know how to behave.

You know what keeps me going everyday? I find it interesting that with every head of hair you need to pluck, you have to adapt and find your own technique. There's thin hair, thick hair, curly hair, all types. And we've got a different type of tweezer for every different kind of hair. And you know what? After all this plucking, I've come up with a theory. I can guess someone's character from the type of hair they have. Thick-haired people? They're hard-headed [*laughs*].

My dreams [*laughs*]? I've only been here a year, so it's a little early for me to start thinking about other jobs. I used to take English classes in the evening, and I'm thinking of starting them again. These days, just about every job requires a foreign language. Mainly though, I dream about the family I'll have some day. My dad owns a motorbike repair shop, so maybe one day after I get married, my husband and I will open our own motorbike repair shop [*sighs and smiles*].

Hanoi, September 2010
Nguyễn Thị Thao, Nguyễn Thúy Linh, Lan Ngo, Jeremy De Nieva

chapter 13
PLAYING

ball boys

HOÀNG. I'm 17 years old and I've been working here for four years.

DUY. I'm also 17. I've been a ball boy for seven months.

HOÀNG. Our job is pretty simple: we pick up tennis balls for customers who come to play tennis.

DUY. Well, sometimes we do other things like pick up trash and wash the courts, but that's not our main job.

HOÀNG. It's really easy, we walk around the court and use this trash scooper to pick up the balls and put them in that box [*points to a large cardboard box that used to contain bottled water*]. If people need balls, we throw them some. Our boss usually brings out the water and talks to the customers about paying for the court. On a normal day, I work about six hours until around 11 p.m., seven days a week. In the mornings, I go to school and then come to the courts after.

DUY. You don't go to school! Don't listen to him [*laughs*]. Kids like us from poor families don't go to school. I stopped going to school in my first year of high school.

HOÀNG. Well, anyway, tennis is my favorite subject [*laughs*]. We play tennis together when people aren't here, just for fun. We get paid 1.5 million đồng [$75] per month so we buy our own food from local restaurants. The rest of my money I spend on going out.

DUY. Me, after work, I go home and sleep. Right now, I live with my mother and father in Hanoi, but our home village in Thái Nguyên is about 80 kilometers north of here.

HOÀNG. I don't go back to my village in Phú Thọ too often. It's a four-hour drive from here, so I stay with family in Hanoi. My parents are just happy that I've been able to get a job and make a living at the tennis courts.

DUY. I normally work eight hours a day and play the rest of the time. There aren't a lot of customers early in the day because it's too hot, so I come here and play, sleep, watch TV, or eat. There's nothing else to do. Then the courts are always busy from 2 to 10 p.m. and we have to work the entire time. Our customers are pretty wealthy. It costs them 60,000 đồng [$3] for one hour per person to play, and then they have to pay for water and for us ball boys. So everything comes up to about 100,000 đồng [$5] per person. Our customers all drive nice cars and motorbikes though, so it's not like it's expensive for them. Most of the customers are older men who come at the same time every week. Sometimes I see foreigners here, like that Indian guy. He's supposed to be the president of some big company. I've never seen a woman play here.

HOÀNG. I like working with my friends here. I don't need or want to do anything else. I don't care about going to university. I don't want to do another job. I like tennis and picking up balls. That's what I'm going to do for the rest of my life ... although it would be nice to live as a professional tennis player. The player I like most is [Rafael] Nadal, but I know I'll never be that good; I just play for fun.

DUY. This job is good for me right now. I don't have any dreams of doing anything else. Why would I? Besides, I like the work just fine. We don't need any equipment, we'll never be replaced by some expensive machine, and our customers don't yell at us for not doing our job. I'm happy with how things are now. Well, I guess it would be nice to get paid more [*laughs*].

Hanoi, September 2010
Đoàn Hồng Hải, Nguyễn Hải Yến, Tina Ngo, Peter Del Moral

bar manager

I don't know how people find out about the bar. It must be the name. When we first opened, some of the foreign customers asked us, "Do you know what 'Golden Cock' means?" When we chose the name of the bar, we just thought it meant "golden rooster," but I guess people came thanks to the other meaning.

I didn't start the bar; my father did in 1993. At first he called it the "Golden Cock," but he had to change it to "GC" because the government didn't allow businesses to use foreign names back then. My father never thought the bar would serve the gay community. It just happened. He simply decided to open the bar because there weren't very many bars in Hanoi back in 1993, and some of his foreign friends thought it would be a good idea. So the GC was actually one of the first bars to open in Hanoi. Back then, eight out of ten customers were foreigners, but this started changing three or four years ago. Now, eight out of ten customers are Vietnamese.

Previously, I studied at the Aviation Academy in Ho Chi Minh City. I only started managing the bar in 2006 when my parents were getting old. I'll have to stop working here too when I get older. A middle-aged woman shouldn't be working at a bar. I have a younger brother who's still in school. He's already working here as a DJ, so he'll probably take over the business eventually. I never had any intention to manage the bar. To tell you the truth, I want to go back to working in a travel agency.

The GC is open every day from 6 to 11:30 p.m. I used to work for a travel agency during the day, so I had to wake up at 6 a.m, work the whole day, and then be at the GC by 6 p.m. It was exhausting, so I ended up giving up the job at the travel agency. Nowadays, I can get up late and take care of whatever little things need to be done before I go to work at the bar. I have ten employees; they're all students so they go to school during the day and work here at night. I don't need to tell employees about the bar before I hire them because they already know about it. Everyone knows this bar. For 17 years, it's stayed the same, and people like that.

The best part of this job is the money. I don't really have a least favorite part of the job. Vomit? Yeah, I guess I don't like the vomit. People throwing up, causing a ruckus, getting into fights, it's all pretty normal. But I never let anything get out of hand. In general, people value the bar and don't want to cause trouble.

Memorable moments? No, every day is the same. After we close the bar I usually go to Solace [a late-night bar] or go eat something with some of the employees and customers. It's a lot of fun. For example, I get so bored during Tết when we close the bar and I have to stay home. I miss the bar.

We have customers of all ages. Lots of regulars too. When I hang out with them, I just have fun. I don't want to dig too deep into their personal lives. Some of my friends are gay or lesbian. They're more fun to hang out with than my straight friends. They're much more open. I've worked here for three or four years now, so it's pretty easy for me to recognize gay people. It's in how they dress, how they talk; some people are just pretty open about it. People aren't embarrassed to be themselves at the GC. Here, ten out of ten people know each other. It's like family here.

I don't have any prejudice against our gay customers. But there is one thing I don't like: when a customer already has a family. I don't like the fact that they deceive their wives. Vietnamese society is pretty conservative, and most people still have trouble accepting homosexuality. Me, I think that Vietnamese society should be more accepting of same-sex relationships. That would mean that fewer women will end up being deceived.

What if my own child was gay? I've never thought about that. Actually, I don't think any parent wants that. Nobody wants their child to turn out that way. I'm not ready to accept it. Anyway, I don't want to get married now; I'm still young and I want to go out and have fun.

Hanoi, November 2010
Nguyễn Thị Thao, Nguyễn Thúy Linh, Lan Ngo, Jeremy De Nieva

karaoke bar owner

My name is Dũng. I'm 34 years old. I work as a P.E. instructor at the university and I also run a karaoke bar on Tây Sơn Street. It used to belong to a friend of mine, but for various reasons he had to sell it and I ended up buying it from him. That was in 2009.

I guess the main reason I bought it was because of our close friendship: I really wanted to help him out. But I also kind of liked the business; I used to come here back when he still owned it just to observe how it worked. But even though I liked it, I still hesitated. Honestly, I was nervous about owning such a sensitive kind of business. You know, seeing as how I'm a teacher and the second job involves dealing with some of the less respectable aspects of society and such. But even so, he was my friend and he was in trouble, so how could I not help him out?

I have to hide this work from a lot of people. For example, my parents and my brothers don't know I own a karaoke bar, but my wife and son do. As for my colleagues at the university, I've only told a handful. But outside of the university and my family, I have to tell people because I need to market the bar. How else are they going to know to come here when they've got a party or a birthday? To succeed in this business, you really have to make use of a wide social network. If I'd paid more attention to networking when I first started out I would be doing a lot better now.

I don't spend much time at the bar myself; I usually just go at the end of the day or on weekends. I hired a manager to take care of all the everyday business. I put in a camera surveillance system too, but I found it wasn't really necessary. Almost all the management and staff are relatives or close acquaintances and they report to me regularly. It's good to have people you know instead of outsiders working for you. It's safer and it's good for your revenue too. And let's be honest, the money is a big part of why

I'm in this business. Even if it can be tiring, it pays better than my civil servant salary at the university, I can tell you that!

Before we moved to Tây Sơn Street, the bar was in a more urban area. It would get really crowded after midnight, but the law requires all bars to close by 1 a.m. So I had to build good relationships with the locals, both the neighbors and the authorities, for us to be able to stay open late. Once I did, though, the bar started to bring in very high returns because of its good location and the way the demand for entertainment just keeps growing and growing.

Location shapes the business in other ways, too: low-end bars work well in areas with lots of universities, while in the downtown area high-end bars are going to be more successful. It's funny, though, but competition really doesn't factor much into the bar's success. This kind of business is so dodgy that I just don't have the time or the energy to worry about what my competitors are up to.

Honestly, this job has brought more bad memories than good ones. People tend to go to karaoke in the evening after they've been eating and drinking, and that can get messy. You get quarrels among guests or between guests and the staff. Sometimes people in the same party scramble for the mic, or they're drunk and they just start a fight for no reason. When that happens, we have to call 113 [the police emergency number], or we have to try to kick them out of the bar ourselves to avoid the hassle of calling the cops. Then there are the times when guests come into the bar and start doing drugs — that can be real trouble. You've just got to know how to handle situations like these if you want to be in this business.

The worst time involved a group that came in at three in the morning. They finished singing around 5 a.m., went down to the reception, and made all the staff line up. My people thought they were just going to pay the bill and give out some tips, but they were wrong. Instead, they slapped each one of the employees and then proceeded to trash the place. We couldn't call 113 either because we were open past the legal operating hours. We just had to stand there and let them go without paying for anything.

But all that aside, I find that this business is just like any other. I mean, all we're doing is providing a service for customers: why can't it be respectable? I know that nowadays, whenever someone hears the term "karaoke bar" or "massage shop" they automatically think it's less than wholesome, but problems like these can happen in any business if the management doesn't work effectively and ethically. The way I see it, if karaoke bar owners run their business honestly and successfully, then they're just as worthy of respect and honor as anyone else out there.

Hanoi, October 2011
Minh Thu Diep, Phạm Phương Thảo, Sean Decker, Huỳnh Đình Quang Minh

mama–san

You could say I come from a "political" family. Half of my family members are Party members. My grandpa is a Party member. My uncle is a Party member. My mom is one as well. My uncle was the head of an office in the Judicial Department, and mom, she used to be an army officer. But her daughter is — this is so funny — a mama-san. Everyone in the family works for the state, and here I am doing this disgraceful job. It's unbelievable, isn't it?

It was totally by chance that I ended up doing this job. It was after I got divorced from my husband. I was in shock. You see, I was rich before I got married. Only 21 years old, and I already had properties and cars. Actually it was my ex-boyfriend who helped me get started. Basically, I got rich playing the real estate market. You could make so much money so fast. Then I met this guy and we got married. Turns out he liked to gamble, and within just a few years after we got married, he'd lost everything we had.

I'd stopped working when I had my son. But after the divorce I had to find some way to make money. I tried this and that but nothing worked out. Then one day I met a girlfriend I hadn't seen for a long time. You know, I wasn't famous or anything before I got married, but I was somebody: I owned property, and I could hold my head up high when I went out. But the day I met my friend in this nice bar in Saigon, I was broke. I had nothing left. When she heard what had happened, she told me about this job managing a karaoke bar. I applied for it and I got it.

So there I was, 25 years old, a single mom, and suddenly I'm supposed to manage more than 100 girls. And they don't wear name tags. I just had to remember their faces. I was petrified at the thought of making a mistake and then the girls wouldn't be afraid of me anymore. I knew that they'd just walk all over me if they could find a single weak spot. And if I made mistakes with the clients, they would get mad and then I'd get in trouble with the boss. It felt like I'd been thrown into a jungle. I was afraid of everyone and everything: the boss, the clients, the girls. But it's funny, I wasn't afraid of the police. I guess I was too busy being afraid of everyone else. But as time went on, the fear wore off. And after six years working there, I was afraid of nothing and no one: not the girls, not the boss, not clients, not the police. No one.

I'd start work at seven every evening. By the time I got there, all the girls had to have finished their make-up and be ready for work. By midnight, it was time to give the clients their bills and start closing up. We'd be closed by 1 a.m. at the latest. Think about it: five hours of work per day. And during the day, I could go shopping, do chores around the house, take my son to school and pick him up. It was perfect.

The bar was in an upmarket hotel, so almost all our clients were foreigners. Sometimes they were travelling for business, but they were mainly working in Saigon. The manager was Korean, so the majority of the clients were Korean businessmen. Other than that, there were some Japanese and a few others. But mostly Koreans. There were some lovely clients. What do I mean by "lovely?" Well, I guess "lovely" means they don't make trouble. But I mean it, some were really nice. I was good at my job, and they'd appreciate it when I already knew what they wanted. Of course, you have to understand that when a man pays a lot of money, he expects to be able to demand certain things; they want this particular girl, they want a discount on this or that. But I knew how to talk to them sweetly, how to persuade them, and how to strike a compromise. Really, they were lovely.

The bar had 21 karaoke rooms and 139 girls. I had to memorize their faces, their names, and their numbers. We didn't call them by their names, we used numbers. I was good: I knew right away if a girl skipped work. I never had to check the attendance book. But that was what the job was all about. A client comes and gets escorted by Ms. A, for example. Then two weeks later, he comes back and says, "I want the same girl as last time." It was my job to know exactly who he was with, and to make sure she was sitting next to him in his karaoke room within minutes, pouring his drinks and laughing at his jokes.

A karaoke bar isn't a brothel, you know. I'd never let my girls do anything sexual in the bar; that's the number one rule. Strictly speaking, the bar employs the girls as professional entertainers, with contracts and everything. So if we ever had any trouble with the police, I'd show them the contracts and the rest of their papers and say, "The bar employs these girls to entertain our clients. How

am I supposed to know what they do in their free time?" That's
in theory, anyway, but at the bar where I worked there'd been a
mama-san who'd had to go to jail for five years. Lots of mama-sans
get caught.

That's one of the reasons I never took a cut from my girls. I
know you don't believe me, but really, I'm telling you the truth.
We all know that mama-sans always take a commission from their
girls. You're crazy not to. Your career isn't long, and you never
know when you're going to get arrested, beat up, or even killed.
So why not make the most of it while you can? Other mama-sans
I know of were making more than 100 million [$5,000] a month.
Even after six years working as a mama-san, I was earning less than
half of that.

Some of the girls called me a coward for not demanding a
cut. But the way I see it, I was just being smart. When you're a
mama-san, the girls already hate your guts; why give them reason
to hate you even more? Do I want a girl squealing to the police if
she gets arrested? And if I take money from her, she becomes my
responsibility. Do I want her calling me at three in the morning
when she's been arrested and needs someone to bail her out? I just
wanted to keep things as nice and simple as possible. I told myself
it wasn't worth being greedy now just to end up paying it all back
later in jail.

The hotel where I was working at actually had two karaoke
bars. The one upstairs where anyone could go, and my bar
downstairs. The one downstairs was the exclusive one: you'd never
know about it unless someone introduced you to it. There was this
one time, after I'd been working for a few years, when the police
raided the bar upstairs. In the middle of the raid, one of the girls
upstairs calls to warn me. I didn't freak out. I knew it was too late
to do anything for them, all I could do was take care of my clients
and my girls. I went straight to the boss and told him: "The cops

are upstairs, we've got to get the bills paid and everyone out of here immediately." Then while he got the money from the clients, I told all the girls to go get changed and get out. It's funny, but I wasn't scared even for a second.

They arrested everybody in the bar upstairs. It was all over the papers. None of my friends or family knew there were two bars in the hotel, so they all thought I'd been arrested. The newspapers even printed the name of the mama-san upstairs, Thảo. One of my little sisters texted me, really worried: "Where are you? Who is Thảo?" Another friend of mine was working as a police detective. He wasn't involved in the raid, but he called me as soon as he heard about it to make sure I was okay.

I took a break for six months after that. Yeah, the cops only arrested people from the bar upstairs, but they later interrogated two of my girls. The girls told the truth about me, they told the cops I didn't know anything about what they did in their off-hours. But still, now the police knew about me. My friend in the criminal branch told me that they had a file on me with my photo and everything. He said it would be best if I laid low for a while, so I did.

Was I close to any of the girls? No. You know, there should always be a distance between a mama-san and her entertainers. But you have to understand them to manage them. So I always wanted to maintain a certain connection with them. It's not like we were close, but I still wanted them to feel comfortable with me, to know it was okay to just have a chat. So sometimes when the girls invited me out, okay, I'd go. It was a way for me to know how they were doing and what was going on. But when it comes to work, you always have to keep some distance. I'd hang out with them, but still, they had to be afraid of me. I was their mama-san.

Let me tell you the truth, the relationship between a mama-san and her girls is usually terrible. I knew of mama-sans who had to quit their job because their girls jumped them and beat them up. On the other hand, I tried to use kindness to run my girls; except when they broke the rules, that is. Then they got exactly what they deserved. But other than that, I was never intentionally mean to them. Plus, it didn't hurt that I never took any money from them. But I know some of them still hated me. Think about it: how can a working girl and her mama-san ever get along, really? It's no different than the relationship between a stepmother and her stepdaughter. But other girls, they loved me. There's this one girl I'll always remember. When she heard I was quitting, she came running out of the karaoke room, hugged me and cried, "Madam, why are you quitting? Don't leave me!"

I started working as a mama-san in 2004 when I was 25, and I retired when I was 31. I didn't expect to last that long in the business. But I did. I think it was my fate. People couldn't believe a mama-san could be so young. Or that I could run so many girls. Usually a mama-san runs 50 girls. I ran 139. I'm proud of that.

There's another thing I'm proud of. I never serviced a client. It's common for mama-sans to service special clients. Let's face it: it's a good way to make extra money. But me, I never even had a drink with a client. It was common for clients to ask me to join them, but I never agreed. There was one regular client who was really persistent, he even talked to the owner privately to have him pressure me to have a drink with him. But I refused, and the owner just had to accept it. If he'd tried to force me, I'd have quit, and he knew he could never find a better mama-san. To tell you the truth, I was pretty famous. Why was I famous? I guess it's because I always smiled. Things went well, I smiled. Things went wrong, I apologized and smiled. I'd hold it in until I could get to the bathroom to cry. The boss saw me once. But I never cried in front of clients, I never showed any emotion in front of clients. When you think of mama-sans, you think they must be tough as nails, don't you? But a mama-san is just as vulnerable as any other woman. But I was always professional in public. I was always the mama-san.

No one in my family knew about my job except my mom. My mom is my best friend. I share everything with her. But I didn't let her tell anyone else. What if my father and others in the family had known? I don't know. I can't even imagine. All I know is that I'm so glad they never published my picture in the newspaper. They published my boss's picture once, though. After I left, the bar was busted and they closed it down.

Before I started working as a mama-san, I thought of working girls as bad, "damaged" girls. This job really changed my thinking. It taught me not to make judgments, and try to put myself in other people's shoes instead. Now I try to understand where people are coming from. These girls were just going to work, doing their job. They weren't hurting anybody. It was their profession. And it cost them sweat, tears, and even blood.

Will I tell my son his mom once worked as a mama-san? Maybe I will .... No, I can't tell him everything. What I can do is try to talk about it in a way that helps him stop judging and open his mind to different people, show him that you should try to understand people first, and even if you can't understand, then you should still sympathize with them ... something like that. So I guess I'll tell him, but I won't give him details. I'll just tell him what I need to give him a better perspective on life, to educate him. But I won't tell him what I did, or how much I earned, or what my girls were like. I can't tell him that.

What if one day my son fell in love with a working girl? Well, have you ever heard of the saying "Some may want a whore to be their wife, but no one wants their wife to be a whore?" There, I said it. No mother wants their son to marry a working girl. Maybe I'll change my mind though. Maybe if she was a sex worker in the past, I wouldn't mind it. Only the present matters, and how she behaves towards other people now. The thing I'd really need to know is whether she truly loves my son.

If a friend of mine wanted to become a mama-san, I'd say: "Yeah, go ahead." It's a profession. I won't stop her. The important thing is to keep a good head on your shoulders, and be tough enough. I'll be honest with you. When I first moved to Singapore a few years ago so my son could go to school here, I saw a classified ad in the papers. Of course it didn't say "mama-san" but "karaoke bar manager." But I looked at it and knew immediately. It was obvious. And I was tempted. For all those years I'd been making good money, and now suddenly I was in this new country and couldn't even get a job. I even tried applying. The only problem was I didn't have papers to work in Singapore legally. For now, I don't really have a plan for the future. I've got savings, I can take care of myself and my son. And I know that whatever comes, I'll adapt, I'll be okay.

Singapore, March 2012
Mai Huyền Chi, Gerard Sasges

hotel receptionist

I'm 22 years old and I just graduated from the Faculty of International Studies at Hanoi University. I used to work at a hotel in the Old Quarter. I started working there when I was in the fourth year of college. I took the job for the extra cash. I wanted to be more independent of my parents and have more opportunities to hang out with my friends.

Officially, my position was "hotel receptionist," but I called myself "The Night Watchman." I worked the night shift from 9:30 p.m. to 7:30 a.m. Basically, I kept track of the customers who came in and out. I made sure they were safe and that everything was working right. Even though it was a part-time job for me, I still ended up working like it was full-time. The cool thing about the job was that I was allowed to sleep after 12:30 a.m.

Working at the hotel allowed me to meet a lot of foreigners. Being an International Studies major was actually useful because I had to interact with people from so many different countries. It gave me the opportunity to learn about other cultures and even to understand my own culture better.

Most foreigners were pretty nice to me. The Germans, the French guys ... actually, all the Europeans were really nice. The only one I didn't like was this one Middle-Eastern guy. It's not because he was Middle-Eastern, it's just that I couldn't understand his English [laughs]. Same with the Chinese. They can't speak any English at all! I remember one time, this Chinese guy was trying to tell me something. I think he wanted food, maybe [laughs]. It can be really frustrating when you can't communicate with people, even when you're face-to-face.

But the majority of our customers were Vietnamese. Most foreigners backpack around Vietnam so they don't want to or just don't have the money to pay for a hotel.

This job definitely wasn't the hardest job I've ever had, but still, it was difficult sometimes. First, there were the weird foreigners I couldn't understand. Another annoying thing was when people went out late and then came back at around 2 or 3 a.m. I'd have to wake up, unlock the door, and let them in. A lot of times they'd be drunk, and I'd just have to put up with it. Then there were customers who'd do a runner and leave without paying. That happened a couple times as well.

Working in a hotel, one gets to see a lot of shady stuff. We'd get drug dealers sometimes, but how am I supposed to know what's going on in the room? Then there's the problem of extra guests. The law in Vietnam says that no one can stay in a hotel room without being checked in. But of course people bring guests back to their room without checking them in, and I guess we just had to make exceptions. Most of the hookers we had coming into the hotel were very young, like high school students.

We'd get a lot of businessmen staying here at the hotel on company trips. You know, they're away from home, they want to have some fun. Of course, the company's paying for the room, not them. So they'd tell me to charge everything to the room, including their hookers.

And then of course there're husbands cheating on their wives and wives cheating on their husbands. You'd also get high school students renting a room just for a couple hours. It seems like some of them are already pretty used to going to hotels. I honestly didn't care about these high school kids having sex. My job was just to get them a room. Attitudes towards love and sex have changed a lot. For a lot of young people these days, sex before marriage just isn't a big deal anymore.

I was getting paid 2.5 million đồng [$125] a month. Sometimes a group would leave a tip too. It was always really random, but on average I could make an extra 400,000 [$20] a week. When you're only making a few million đồng like that, a hotel receptionist is always going to be looking for ways to make a little more money. Okay, steal a little more money, I guess [*laughs*]. The hotel was actually owned by my aunt, so of course I never did it. But there are lots of ways the other employees could make money, like not recording the guests who are only there for a few hours, or taking some of the money we charge for taxi fees.

I worked at the hotel for a year. It was the same thing over and over again. Every day was the same. Actually, I didn't even ask to work there; my aunt kind of forced me to. So it's not like I wanted to make it my career or anything. It was just something to do for a couple of years so I could make some money. Now I've got a new job that I like a lot better. Especially because I finally have time to sleep [*laughs*].

Hanoi, September 2011
Hoàng Minh Trang, Mai Nguyen, Loc Le, Nguyễn Huy Anh

chapter 14

TEACHING
& LEARNING

kindergarten teacher

My name is Trang. I'm 24 years old, and I work as a kindergarten teacher and an at-home tutor. I'm also a part-time university student specializing in preschool education.

I'm always busy because I have lesson plans to prepare and errands to run. I have to wake up at 6 a.m. just to fit everything into the day. I make sure I squeeze in some time to exercise every morning when I wake up, and then I hop into the shower. Once I get dressed and eat breakfast, I head to the school, which is about a ten-minute motorbike ride from my apartment. My family's originally from Hưng Yên, but these days I live in Hanoi and my dad and brother live in Sơn La, so I'm pretty far from family.

After lunch, when all the other teachers get to take a nap, I have to stay awake to prepare lesson plans for everyone. I've been teaching and managing the curriculum for the teachers like this for three years now, and I find it really rewarding. Aside from my responsibilities as a teacher, I've also kind of taken over the management of parent-teacher relations. If there are any concerns or problems that need to be addressed, I'm there.

I never thought I'd end up here. When I was growing up, my mom wanted me to become a kindergarten teacher, but I never really considered it. Then she passed away seven years ago and — even though many of my friends discouraged me — I decided to become a kindergarten teacher in remembrance of her. When I have troubles and feel stressed out, I think of my mom and write everything down in my diary. I ask my mom, "What should I do now, mom?" and she seems to be near me. Sometimes, I read over all the pages I've written to my mom and feel sad, but really, she's become a big part of my motivation to keep going.

I think that one of the most important parts of being a kindergarten teacher is being carefully and thoroughly trained. Secondly, you should be patient and passionate about the job. And finally, you have to be able to take a lot of stress; this job comes with a lot of pressure — pressure from the school, pressure from the kids, and especially pressure from the parents.

The best part of my job is the fact that I get to play with kids. Each child is different and has a unique personality, but I've never met a kid who doesn't love to draw. One loves to draw smiley faces, while another loves to draw houses and toys. They're all so precious and letting them draw expands their imagination.

I remember my first day at the kindergarten. I'd decided to teach the kids a new song called "Cá vàng" [goldfish]. I thought that it'd be fun to bring a goldfish to class. As soon as I brought the goldfish out, none of the kids paid any attention to me anymore, all they could see was that little fish. It got to a point where I had to yell so loudly that I lost my voice. By the time I finally got everyone calmed down again, it was time for the kids to go home, and I never got to teach them the song [*laughs*].

You don't earn much working as a kindergarten teacher. It covers my tuition and meals, but there's no way I'll ever have money to burn. And even if I did have money, I wouldn't have time to spend it. My days are filled with teaching, and because we're a private kindergarten, we don't get a lot of vacation days. Instead of two months like at the state schools, I only have one week off during the summer. If I have some days off, I go for a trip with my friends. Last year I went to Cửa Lò, and this year, my colleague and I took a quick trip to the beach at Sầm Sơn.

Personally, I wouldn't want my kids doing the same job as me. It's not easy, and you need a lot of patience and commitment. I have to work all day, and have little time for myself, let alone my family. But in the end, if my kids decide that they want to be kindergarten teachers like their mom, by all means; I'll support them. It's their future, not mine. The important thing is that they have the freedom to choose the career they want.

I've been part of this kindergarten ever since I got out of college, and working here has allowed me to mature tremendously. But I know I've still got a lot of weaknesses I need to address and skills and knowledge that I need to learn before I can think of leaving this job. I don't have any specific goals, I'm just going to take things as they come and be open to trying new things. I've never really thought of being the head of the kindergarten, but who knows? Like everyone, I've got dreams and aspirations; I want a job that gives me a good salary and social status. But maybe once people understand how hard it is to be a kindergarten teacher, and think about the importance of the formative years of their child's education, they'll start to appreciate the value of what we do. That's the most important thing.

Hanoi, September 2010
Đoàn Lê Thoa, Kathy Nguyen, Andrew Marvin, Đỗ Thu Hiền

elementary schoolteacher

I used to be shocked when I came to class and not a single student showed up. Not anymore [*laughs*]. Some people say teaching is an easy job; all you need to do is prepare a lesson plan, put on nice clothes and walk to class. But you've got no idea how hard teaching is unless you try it yourself, especially teaching in a mountainous region.

I'm Nam and I'm 35 years old. I'm a teacher in Yên Bái province. I'm married and we have one daughter. My wife is also a teacher. She teaches at the high school in town. I've been a teacher for 14 years and have been teaching at this school for 5 years now. Before this, I taught at two other schools closer to town. This school is the furthest from town. The roads here are pretty bad, and getting here from town isn't easy, so during the week I stay at the school teachers' dormitory. I only go home to see my family on weekends.

When I first moved here, I'd already mentally prepared myself for the worst, but even so, I still wanted to give up [*laughs*]. At that time, the school only had a few classrooms. The walls were made from bamboo covered with mud. There was no electricity. The blackboards were in poor condition, the tables and chairs were damaged. The roofs were thatched with palm leaves, the floors were slippery. We didn't have cement floors like we do now. On sunny days, things were okay. But on rainy days, teachers and students would slip and fall one after the other, as if the floors were covered with banana peels. During the winter, teachers' and students' faces would actually turn purple from the cold. In short, life was very hard.

Now, things have improved. Students come to class more often. The government has built better school facilities, and the number of teachers has increased. But the most important thing

is that we've got electricity now! You have no idea how happy we
were the day we got electricity! The happiness was indescribable!

Most of the teachers here are from either the nearby town or
other districts in the province. We're all very close. You've got
to stick together when you're in the middle of nowhere like this,
you know? Without each other's support, we wouldn't be able to
survive here.

About 98 per cent of the students at the school are from one
of the ethnic minority groups. Most of them are Dao [Yao]. In
the old days, they didn't like coming to class, and we had very
few students. We often had to travel across mountains and rivers
to their houses to encourage them to come to class. Many parents
didn't want to send their kids to school because, the way they saw
it, they didn't even have enough food to eat, so why send their kids
to class if it wouldn't make their stomachs full? We had to work
really hard to change their thinking and convince them that it was
important. Also, most of the students here don't speak Kinh [the
language of the ethnic Vietnamese majority] so all the teachers
here have to learn the local languages. We teach in the minority
languages first and then gradually teach in the national language.
We all joke that while everyone else learns English or Korean
so they can go abroad, us teachers up here are learning Dao and
Hmong to "go domestic" [*laughs*].

Like in other places, classes here start at 7:30 a.m. But the
problem is that the sun rises later in the mountains, so there's no
light out until about 8 or 9 a.m. We only teach in the mornings,
because there aren't enough classes to divide the school into
morning and afternoon shifts. Kids who live far away can stay in
the school dorm. Before we had electricity, we had to finish all our
work before sunset. At night, we only had an oil lamp so there
was just enough light to move around. I'm a guy so it wasn't a
big deal, but the women teachers were scared to go to the toilet at

night because it gets so dark and the toilet is far from the dorm.

The school I teach at is one of the schools included in Policy 135 [a government policy intended to support development in remote regions], so I get paid more than the teachers in town. But in town, teachers can teach outside classes to earn more money [a reference to an officially illegal but still widespread practice used by teachers in wealthier areas to supplement their low official salaries]. Here, no student wants to study extra hours. So my extra job is raising chickens and tending the garden [*laughs*]. Right now, I've got a flock of about 50 chickens. Every time a brood grows old enough, I send some chickens home to my parents, relatives and friends as gifts, and bring some home to my wife. The rest I sell in the market, and they actually bring in a decent amount of money. I also have vegetables from the garden and I can catch fish in the rivers. Actually my food situation is pretty good: I always eat fresh, safe food; no need to worry about harmful chemicals like folks in the city [*laughs*].

There are many things you have to get used to when you're teaching here [*laughs*]. Like coming to class on a rainy day only to face an empty classroom. Then, no one shows up when it's a sunny day either. After a while, I learned that ethnic minorities have "time-out days." "Thunder time-out day," "wind time-out day," "tiger time-out day," the list goes on. On those days, people won't step out of their houses. There's nothing you can do because it's their custom and you need to respect that. Even if you want to change it, things have got to be done gradually.

To be honest, it would be great if I could teach in town, but I know that's probably not going to happen anytime soon. Anyway, life here is still good. The path of bringing literacy and knowledge to children here is long and difficult, but all you can do is try your best [*laughs*]. I just hope that the government will start to give a higher priority to the people here. We dream of the day when our students can walk to school on nice paved roads, not these rugged rocky paths [*sighs*].

Vĩnh Sơn, November 2011
Lena Tran, Maya Weir, Nguyễn Thùy Trang, Vũ Thu Hiền

calligrapher

I grew up in Nghệ An, a province in Central Vietnam with a long tradition of scholarship. I was lucky to grow up in a household where my father taught me Chinese characters. No classroom; just a mat to lie on while I practiced. When I didn't execute the characters well, he'd spank me. But I really loved learning new characters. To this day, I still have a passion for calligraphy.

I was in the army for 18 years from 1950 to 1968, fighting first against the French, then the Americans. However, my job wasn't to hold a rifle and shoot people. Actually, they sent me to learn Russian and then assigned me to work as an interpreter. I mainly accompanied the Soviet specialists who were here to help train Vietnamese soldiers. After I retired from the army, I taught Russian at the Foreign Trade University for 20 years. I retired from the university at the age of 63 and I've devoted myself to my calligraphy ever since.

After I retired, I gave away all of my Russian books and replaced them with books that would help me improve my calligraphy. I'd spend whole days and nights reading and practicing; sometimes I wouldn't go to bed until 11 p.m. During the summer, I'd take a mat outside and lie there wearing just my shorts, devouring a stack of books [*laughs*]. My wife, who's always trying to get me to take care of my health, she said to me, "You're so funny these days: you never worked this hard or stayed up this late when you were still working!"

Besides being a calligrapher, I also write articles for the Hán-Nôm Institute [for the study of Vietnamese documents written in Hán [classical Chinese characters] and Nôm [Vietnamese characters] before the adoption of the Vietnamese alphabet in the early twentieth century]. After all my years studying, I'm not just a scholar of classical Chinese, but Nôm as well. I've actually just finished a new translation of Truyện Kiều [a classic of Vietnamese literature written in Nôm verse by Nguyễn Du in the early 1800s]. The hard part wasn't translating Nôm to Quốc ngữ [the modern Vietnamese alphabet]: no, that's actually pretty easy. What takes time is the painstaking research and word-for-word comparison of all the different versions of the text that have been published over the years. Altogether, it took me almost a year to finish.

Calligraphy has really flourished in the last ten years. What with the war and everything, for a time, the tradition was almost lost. But as conditions have improved, calligraphy has become popular once again. Take for example the tradition of câu đối [a kind of poetry consisting of parallel phrases]. It's an old Tết custom for people to ask a calligrapher to write them a câu đối to decorate the home and ensure a good start to the New Year. So as Tết gets closer, you'll find calligraphers setting up stalls in different places around the city, like the Vân Hồ exhibition center.

Văn Miếu [loosely translated as "Temple of Literature", which honors Confucius and others central to the scholarly tradition in Vietnam] is another place where you can find calligraphers. Students go with their parents to ask for characters that will help them do well in school or pass the university entrance

exam. Nobody knows for sure if it helps, but I guess it can't hurt [*laughs*]! Then you have your young folks who get calligraphy as a gift for their lovers.

It's actually a wonderful part of Vietnamese culture, the tradition of writing auspicious characters, but it's such a shame, the way it's become so commercialized nowadays. A lot of people call the Temple of Literature a "calligraphy supermarket." Before, you would never use the words "buy" or "sell" when talking about a piece of calligraphy. But these days, people bargain over them like they're buying a piece of fish in the market.

Not everyone finds calligraphy interesting, even people who study Chinese. Young people these days prefer business; even my own sons [*laughs*]. Both of them studied at the Foreign Trade University, and neither one cares about calligraphy. So as I get older, I worry; when I'm gone, I don't know who will want to inherit the library I've worked so hard to collect.

Calligraphy isn't just about writing beautifully, it's also about gaining a deep understanding of a culture. The only way you can reach that level of understanding is if you have real passion. I don't know how many thousands of brushes I've worn out in order to gain the knowledge and understanding I have now. But I do know that whenever I finish a piece of calligraphy, I feel a deep sense of fulfillment. It's something I never experienced while I was still working. It's something that can never come from a salary, only from a passion for doing something you really love.

Hanoi, September 2011
Tina Bao-Ngan Ngo, Nguyễn Thị Lan, Annelisa Luong, Bùi Hà Phương

buddhist nun

At the pagoda, people call me "Phương Huyền," but the name my parents gave me is "Thu." I'm 27 and I'm from Bình Điền, Huế. My parents are farmers. I have four siblings. I have an older brother who has his own family and house now. Then there's me. Next is my little brother. He used to be a bus driver but now he's a truck driver. And my younger sister, she's a Buddhist nun in Nha Trang.

I've always had an affinity for Buddhism. But it was only in 1999 that I understood it was my calling. That was the year of the bad flood, and all the monks and nuns had come out to help people in the town. I was with Abbess and four sisters at the preschool at Đông Ba market, and we placed all the toys and everything on higher ground to keep them out of the rising water. It was already late at night when the flood stopped so we stayed there at the preschool to sleep. We even had the chance to lie next to Abbess. It was the first time that ever happened. We were all so afraid that the flood would come again; actually, none of us could sleep.

At that time, I still had long, beautiful hair. As I lay next to Abbess, from time to time she would tuck my hair away to keep it from falling into the water. I felt so much love from her. It's hard to describe. I felt like it was like an electric shock running through my body and spreading love through me. That's when I really felt that it was my fate and I became more determined than ever to be a nun. I thought that I could only help my own family if I just stayed at home, got married, had a husband and kids; I wouldn't even have time to help my parents. But if I entered the sangha [the Buddhist community of nuns, monks, and practicing lay people] I could help more people with all my heart. It's already so hard scrambling around, earning a living, not to mention keeping your heart open to helping others. The path of the sangha seemed like a purer way.

My parents understand Buddhism very well, but even so, they were torn when they found out that their daughter had chosen this path. They were happy, but at the same time they didn't like the idea, mainly because life in the pagoda is very difficult. So my family was against it, especially my eldest brother. He didn't even want to see me again after I left home for the pagoda. He said if I stayed home and lived well, then I could help others. But if I chose the path without a husband or children, I would miss out on many things in life. Even though my parents eventually agreed, he was still strongly opposed to it. But I told him, "It's my life, my decision to make, and my own path to choose." Sometimes I go home and he won't even want to see my face. But I also know he gives my mom money to pass to me, so the feelings that exist between a brother and a sister are still there.

Every morning, we get up at 3:15 a.m. We wash up and get ready. Then at 3:30 a.m. the bell rings to mark the start of prayers. We pray until five o'clock, then go downstairs and start the chores; some of us do the cooking, while others do the cleaning or the gardening. At 6:15 a.m., we have breakfast. I leave for school before seven and come back around ten and continue with my chores. After lunch, I usually take a nap until 1:30 or 2 p.m. I'll study until 3:15 p.m., then I do some more chores until dinner at 5 p.m. After dinner we have some free time until prayers. We're allowed to go sleep at nine o'clock, but I usually stay up doing homework till 11:30 p.m. or midnight. I don't get more than five hours of sleep a day.

Since I became a nun and left my family home, I think of everywhere as my home, and of Abbess as my mother; even more than a mother, actually. According to Buddha, parents are simply the ones who give birth to us, while Abbess is the one who guides us to a higher path. Her devotion is even greater than that of a parent's. Then there's the way parents tend to spoil their kids,

unlike Abbess, who can be strict with us when she has to be. So for Abbess, we feel a mix of both respect and love. As for all the other nuns, each of us had to leave our homes to be here, all of us see each other as sisters in one big family now. The older nuns take care of the younger ones — sometimes the younger nuns do something wrong and make us older nuns really mad, but we still show them the way because if we don't, no one will. So in some ways, our relationships are even deeper than the relationships between sisters.

Well, I'm still pretty young now and Abbess takes responsibility for everything, so the only challenge I really have to face is getting up early each morning [*laughs*]. For now, I still don't have to worry about anything. When I'm older, I'll have to go out into the world and fulfill my obligations to society, maybe by teaching in the preschool. But for now, I still feel like I'm a little kid, safe in my parents' arms. I haven't had to face the challenges my older sisters have faced as instructors and headmistresses of the preschool; they have so many responsibilities, like organizing the timetable, salaries, accounting, taking care of the kids .... It's a charity preschool and the fees are really low, so one of the biggest challenges is reaching out to the community for support and persuading the lay instructors to stay despite the low salaries. It's really hard for the older nuns. But I'm still in school myself, so I don't have to worry about that just yet [*laughs*].

After they graduate, some of the nuns stay here to work at the preschool, while others do missionary work, the work of the Lord Buddha, by going to places where they're needed, where the teachings of the Buddha aren't as well known yet. Nuns often go up North to take up positions as abbesses. It's so hard when we first go out into the world. We get used to Abbess taking care of everything, and then suddenly we have to deal with everything ourselves, especially if we find ourselves put in the position of being an abbess.

It's really hard being a nun because we're still human and our desire for pleasure is still strong. Take the four postures [meditation practices of walking, standing, sitting, and lying], for example. We study the rules, but applying them is really hard because they're applicable to everything we do. I still have to practice, even now. Abbess says that I still walk way too fast and that I need to slow down. But sometimes when we have guests, I run because I don't want them to wait; then Abbess scolds me. Things like this aren't easy, but they aren't exactly hard either. Everything gets easier with practice.

If someone was trying to choose between the life of the sangha and the life of the world and they asked me for my opinion, I would advise them to enter the sangha. The path of being a nun or a monk is a difficult one. There are many things to worry about, you can't just follow your desires, and sometimes you get into trouble. But there are times when you feel so peaceful, so safe, so calm. That's why I think the path of the sangha is one of the best paths one can take. The Lord Buddha was a prince who renounced his throne and his riches to discover the path. Now that he's already shown us the path, all we have to do is follow it. So why wouldn't we? It would be such a waste if we didn't [*laughs*]!

Huế, September 2011
Tina Bao-Ngan Ngo, Nguyễn Thị Lan, Bùi Hà Phương, Annelisa Luong

chapter 15

CARING

nurse

My name is Hiền and I was brought up in Vân La village in Hà Tây province [part of the Hanoi metropolitan area since 2008]. I'm 65 years old and I come from a family of ten siblings. I decided go into medicine because I liked the idea of being able to help people.

I started medical school back in 1965 during the war. I was a very hardworking student. Back then, I had to go to school and rescue people from the bombings at the same time. Was I afraid? Oh no. Back then, everyone had to know how to avoid the bombs: you'd know where the shelters were and how to find cover if you got caught out when the bombing started. I always wore a helmet and carried my medical supplies with me in the morning when I went to school. They needed all the medical students' help at that time, so I just did it. It was normal.

That means I didn't grow up in a time of peace like you kids, I grew up in a time of war. You'll never be able to imagine what it was like. This village here was bombed heavily; after a while we considered bombing as normal as eating rice. I remember one day, it was only seven in the morning, when they called me to a place about a kilometer away from the school. When I got there, I just threw my bike down and started helping however I could. There were 36 people killed or injured. One bomb would shatter into a thousand pieces of shrapnel. It was terrible. No number of books can ever contain all those memories.

I began my career as a nurse in 1965 and retired in 2001. In 1965, I started my studies at the intermediate medical school in Hà Tây, then from 1966 to 1968, I studied General Medicine at the Medical School. In 1968, I started working at the community clinic. I specialized in pregnancies and family planning. My duties included prenatal care, emergencies, deliveries, and then immunizations and vaccines for children up to the age of five. At the time of my retirement, I was working as Director of the clinic.

I loved my work. Nothing can compare to the joy of holding a small child in your arms. My favorite part of the job is a peaceful, easy birth where the mother and her child are both healthy. My least favorite part is the plain lack of sleep. But even with all the sleepless nights, I could never dream of taking on any other job. I will always want to have at least one kid among my nieces and nephews embark on this career.

No, I don't have any children of my own. I never wanted a family. I loved a man a long time ago, but he sacrificed his life for the war and I never remarried. It's not like nobody else ever asked for my hand, plenty did. It's just that love was simple for me then; when he died, I could never consider loving someone else.

These two hands of mine have delivered more than 2,000 babies. Out of 2,000, seven were C-sections. About 50 of them were delivered at home. Of course, nobody wants to deliver at home, but back then the only way of getting around was on bicycle or on foot, and sometimes there just wasn't enough time to make it to the clinic. Then there's another 50, well, I delivered them

outside. The mother's water would break while they were out in the fields or somewhere, so someone would call me and off I'd run, through the village, to find the woman who was giving birth.

I'm proud to say that no one has ever died in my hands. But I'll always remember this one case where the mother was having complications. She was quite old, 48 or 49 years old, and was very sick and weak. It was a difficult birth, and we really didn't think she was going to make it. We couldn't believe it when just 30 minutes after her son was born, she looked up at all of us and asked, "So when do we eat?" [*laughs*]. She was fine. Her husband was so surprised and happy. To this day, she's always taught her kids and her grandkids to show me the greatest respect. Her son is more than 30 years old now, but when we meet on the street, she still tells him "You see Grandmother? If it weren't for her, neither one of us would be here."

Hà Tây, September 2010
Jeremy De Nieva, Nguyễn Thị Thao, Nguyễn Thúy Linh, Lan Ngo

masseuse

My name is Hằng. I'm 40 years old, and I've been working as a therapeutic masseuse for 20 years. These days, I own my own business and I only work when we have too many customers for the staff to handle. Before I became a masseuse, I was a construction worker back in my hometown in Thanh Hoá province, but the work really didn't inspire me. Back then, I used to volunteer by helping a masseur who did charity work in the community. The job looking interesting and I liked the idea of helping people so I decided to become a masseuse.

I enrolled in the Tuệ Tĩnh School of Traditional Medicine in Hanoi [today the Vietnam University of Traditional Medicine]. For three years, I studied all the different techniques of traditional medicine like diagnosing patients, using acupuncture, and prescribing different medicines. Then for another three years, I studied Western medicine along with traditional medicine. Finally, I spent three more years specializing in acupuncture. So you see, my training took a total of nine years.

My massage shop is open from eight o'clock in the morning to eleven o'clock at night. I've got seven or eight women working for me now. On average, we get a few dozen clients each day. Usually, I just manage things and collect the money. My employees get a 30 per cent commission. My main job is to train all my employees. I don't train just anyone, only people who are ready to commit to working for my shop. Some people might just learn the techniques and then go work for someone else, you know?

The hardest part — but also the secret to success — is perseverance. Massage has many difficult techniques that take time to learn. Some look easy but you can't just go home and do them yourself. You've got to know the exact location of each nerve. It's really difficult! Some of my employees have already gone through three years of training at the traditional medicine school, but even so, I still have to spend a lot of time and effort training them.

There are some people who quit or I just let them go after two or three days because they can't get used to the workload. They complain that their hands get sore and strained [*laughs*]. I've been doing this for 20 years. Look at how big my hands and wrists are. So manly, right [*laughs*]? However, even my hands are usually sore after each session. But you know, I'm used to it. The most important thing is to pay attention to each technique or else the patients won't get better.

The clients vary. Most of my customers are men. Women are more careful with their money: only wealthy women or women with a specific injury come in for massages. Sometimes, drunk men come in to get massages to increase their blood circulation. After about an hour or so, they're completely sober again. And a lot of clients come straight from work without showering first. I'll tell you, some people have stronger body odor than others, but that's just how this job is.

Sometimes customers expect "extra services" so I have to explain that we don't do that sort of thing at my shop. The working space here is very open. There are people walking back and forth all the time. You should be able to figure that out just from looking at the layout of the shop. But there are other places, like the massage shop behind mine, where they do that sort of thing. The workers there wear short shorts and the massage rooms are private. But you know what? Even at those places, the girls aren't supposed to have sex with their clients. If a client requests it, those girls will give them a hand job or a blow job. But some people don't understand, they think all places are the same, that all massage shops give "happy endings."

This job doesn't allow me any time off. I'm here 24/7 except for when I go to the market or pick up my kids. We don't have a set schedule for lunch or dinner breaks. Whenever a client comes in, we go to work even if we're in the middle of eating. Some days, the clients come in nonstop and it gets really hectic. But we just work until everyone's gone. Just grabbing some food whenever you can isn't good for your health, but there's nothing we can do. Work is work! The only time off we get is when we close for eight days over Tết. But with that many days off, the lost income almost kills me. The lost rent alone is a dozen million đồng [$600]; that's a lot!

Fortunately, my health is really good. I hardly ever get sick. Even after getting married and giving birth to my daughters, I'm still really healthy. If I work too hard, I may get tired, but I never get sick. When I was pregnant with my first daughter, I worked until the day before I went into labor. After she was born, I was off work for one month. Then with my second daughter, I was off for a week. Well, three days to be exact. I remember on the third day, a patient came in with a dislocated shoulder from practicing martial arts and asked me to treat him. I was still really weak so I had to get some of my employees to help too.

Both of my daughters are still really little, so I don't want to expand or open a second shop. When I was young, I didn't even think about dating; men scared me so I focused on my career instead. That's why I didn't get married until I was 36. Now, I want to spend time taking care of my family.

Do I want my kids to follow in my footsteps? Well, I'll tell you a cute story. The oldest is only four years old but she watches my employees while they're working and then tries to imitate what she saw on her dad. The youngest, she's only two, and she also likes to watch and practice along with them when I'm teaching my employees [*smiles*]. But honestly, they're too young to know what they like yet. And what if I plan on them taking over the business, but then it turns out they don't want to? That's not going to do anyone any good. It doesn't matter what your profession is, you've got to love doing it. This job is no exception.

Hanoi, October 2011
Vũ Phương Thảo, Ngoc-Diep Tang, Haven Rocha, Hoàng Huyền Trang

professional carer

My name is Hoa and I'm 52. I'm from Thanh Liêm in Hà Nam.
I've been living in Hanoi for five or six years already. It was really
hard to make a living in my hometown, so I came here to work.
I initially took care of elderly folks in their homes, but many of
them became so ill that they had to be transferred to the hospital. I
preferred the hospital environment, so I followed my patients and
started working there. I decided that this was a career that I could
pursue for a long time. I've worked at practically every hospital in
Hanoi already, but Bạch Mai Hospital is where I work most often.

Regardless of who a patient is — male or female, young or old,
fat or skinny — I accept the job if they hire me. It turns out that
working with men is easier, since it's cleaner when they relieve
themselves. Plus, the male patients here are rarely much younger
than me; the youngest are still around my age. And it's not just
bedridden people who hire me; I have patients who can walk too.
It's just that in Vietnam, no one wants to leave a patient in the
hospital by themselves. What if they have to use the bathroom, eat
a meal, go outside for fresh air, go to physical therapy? So people
hire me when when they have the financial means to do so and
don't have anyone in the family who can take care of the patient.

I look after patients in the hospital everyday. If the patient is
bedridden and can't move, I have to help them when they relieve
themselves. I also have to turn them around from time to time
because if you lie down for long periods of time, your lungs can
close up and you become susceptible to developing sores on your
back and buttocks. Every two hours, I have to turn their body and
pat their back so that mucus doesn't get stuck in their lungs. As
for patients who can still stand and move around, I have to walk
with them everyday to get fresh air and stimulate their minds.

Being a professional carer is a 24-hour-a-day job: I have to be here whenever they're awake. But I still have time to eat and shower, and at night someone in the family usually comes by and takes over for a few hours. So it's not like I have to physically sit by the patient's side all day. The night shift requires two people at the very least, and some families have the financial means to have three carers working shifts. If the patient requires care throughout the night, I can manage the first few nights, but I can't handle it after a while because it's so tiring. After all, I have to care for the patient throughout the day too. It's really strenuous caring for bedridden patients, especially those who are on life support or who have severe brain damage. With conscious patients, I can talk to them and ask them what they need; but with unconscious patients, it's difficult, much more difficult.

With bedridden patients, you usually have to look after all of their eating, health, and personal hygiene needs. And because of that, you can't be afraid of getting your hands dirty or getting infected; all you can do is take preventative measures. There are times when I have to care for HIV-infected patients and drug-addicted patients. But when you know you're dealing with a contagious disease and the ways in which you can get infected as well as the ways to prevent infection, there's really nothing to be afraid of.

If you hired a maid to do this job, they wouldn't be able to do it because this work really requires a skilled professional. For example, patients must be fed every three hours, but before you feed them again you have to check the tube to see if there's still food from the last meal there; you can't keep injecting food into the tube when there's still undigested food in their system. Then when patients are done eating, you have to clean the feeding tube carefully. Milk, porridge, and juice get stuck in there, so it's really important to keep it clean.

After you've done this job for a long time, nothing's really difficult anymore. It's just the new folks who feel like they're fumbling around, because they don't know anything yet. Now that I have the experience, I find it very simple. For example, there are people even smaller than me caring for large patients, but it's not a problem because they know what they're doing. They have to. Otherwise, no one would be able to lift the patients, not even their own family members. We know how to lift the patients and keep the beds clean and tidy; we can't have the doctors reminding us to clean up. We keep the patients as clean as we keep ourselves; after all, we're the ones running the risk of infection and disease.

Doctors and nurses never complain and the patients' relatives are also usually sympathetic, but the patients themselves can be very difficult. There are patients who yell or cuss you out. At times like that, you should keep calm and refrain from raising your voice too. You have to remember it's not easy for them. Then sometimes you get mentally unstable patients who just cuss you out all day. It's not fun, but it's my job and it's the only one I can do.

There are a lot of professional carers like me here. Except for a few newcomers, we all know each other; even when new people come, it just takes one or two jobs for us all to get acquainted. We mainly get customers by word of mouth. I trust that if I do a good job, people will recommend me to their friends and neighbors. Then doctors, nurses, and staff will recommend you too, since new patients and their families often don't know anything when they first arrive at the hospital. Plus, the carers here all know each other and have good working relationships. If I can't take on another patient, I'll refer them to another carer in my group who's dependable and capable.

Normally, the price is fixed and all the carers charge the same daily rate. For patients who are only mildly ill, the family can negotiate beforehand for a lower price. If the patient stays for as long as 20 days to two or three months, my rate is relatively high. A lot of patients stay for so long that they're transferred to another institution, so I follow them there too. My job is usually done after the patient leaves the institution, but some families need me to follow the patient home and continue to care for them. Two years ago, I stayed in Đông Anh to care for the elderly mother of a man who worked in Hanoi. In the hospital, the nurses set up the feeding tubes and the catheters, but in a home I have to do it myself. You really have to know what you're doing in order to work in someone's home.

I get paid 250,000 đồng [$12.50] per day. I arrange my own meals, but sometimes families offer me food, like, "I'll treat you to a meal today," or "Since I'm bringing food for mom, you should eat with her." Otherwise, I pay for myself. I get 7.5 million [$375] for one month with a longer-term patient. Some patients only stay for a week. I try to find another patient right after they leave, but sometimes it takes a whole week before I find the next one. Sometimes an old patient will leave in the morning and a new patient will come in the afternoon; I'll get a double wage that day, but cases like that are rare. Some families give me an extra million [$50] if they think I did a good job, if I was caring, knew what I was doing, and they didn't have to keep an eye on me. But families usually don't worry about these issues for more than the first few days because they know we're all professionals here.

This line of work requires a lot of heart. You have to look at your patients as family so that you care for them with all your heart — that way, you'll never mess up. I've had a lot of cases where my patients passed away. When they start becoming too weak, I have to tell their families so they can watch over the patient with me day and night. Of course I feel sad when a patient passes away. After all, I took care of them and established a relationship with them, especially with the long-term patients.

Sometimes when the family isn't very close to the patient, I'm the one who ends up washing the body, changing the clothes, and taking them to the funeral home. Sometimes, I stay for three or four days while the cremation or burial process goes on. In cases like that, I can say that I really took care of everything for them, from the day they came to the hospital to the day they passed on to the next world.

Hanoi, November 2011
Nguyễn Thị Lan, Bùi Hà Phương, Tina Bao-Ngan Ngo, Annelisa Luong

bone cleaner

Hello everyone, my name's Thanh and I'm 55 years old. I live in Xuân Canh village in Từ Liêm district. I'm semi-retired now; used to work in construction. But that's just one of my jobs [*smiles*]. On the other hand, I'm still doing another job that's not like any other. I'm a bone cleaner. If I had to, I'd put it that way. I'm not really one of those professionals like at Văn Điển or the other cemeteries. I mainly exhume for relatives, neighbors, or other acquaintances who need my help.

I know a lot of people are freaked out by the work I do. One time, when I was being introduced to some new people, I decided to tell them I was a bone cleaner. I wanted to see how they'd react, and it was just as I expected! They grimaced unintentionally, eye contact wasn't natural like before, some of them even choked while eating. Exhuming bodies isn't my main job, but even so, it still hurts to see how people react; it's a decent job, so what's wrong with it? But ever since then, I don't introduce myself as a bone cleaner when I meet new people anymore. It's partly because I don't want my kids to be put in an awkward situation. If adults behave that way, just imagine how kids will react.

My first time exhuming was in 1997; yup, that sounds about right. That was when one of my relatives asked me to exhume a body. I guess everyone in the family thought I was the right age for the job. Because it was for a family member, I accepted. I thought nothing of it — just digging up bones, that's all. But when the grave was finally dug up and I got ready to open the coffin, suddenly I felt freezing cold and both my hands went numb.

I remember those sensations very well, the feeling of facing a different world for the first time, the world of the dead. When I opened the coffin lid and saw the remains inside, suddenly I felt confused, my hands and feet were shaking and I didn't know what to do. Somebody next to me gave me a nudge and I slowly remembered what I'd come there for.

You've got to exhume bones in the right order. You exhume the skull first, then the bones of the left arm, the right arm, the thigh bone and shin bone of the left leg, then the right; after that, each rib bone, and then finally the vertebrae. My job is to climb down into the grave, lift each bone out of the coffin and clean the sediment off with water. Then I give it to someone else standing at the side of the grave, who washes it again with water that's infused with cardamom and cinnamon. After they're all cleaned, we put the bones inside a smaller coffin. By then, my work is pretty much done.

After I exhumed my first body, some other family members asked for my help. Gradually I got more and more familiar with the work. Then word started getting around, so after a certain point — I'm not even sure when — exhuming turned into another job of mine [*smiles*]. My wife, of course, doesn't want me to do this anymore. She wants me to retire completely, but when people ask me, I can't refuse. I do this job to help others, not to make a profit. Usually when I exhume for a close relative, I don't take any money, I just eat the meals they offer me in gratitude. As for other people, I take about 500,000 or 700,000 đồng [$25–$35]. The way I see it, the main thing is to help other people and accumulate merit for future generations.

My wife may not like this job of mine, but she's still very caring. Every time I come home from exhuming a body, she heats up a tub of water with herbs in it for me. This helps get rid of the odor when I bathe. And before I head out, she prepares all my work clothes and gear for me: a raincoat, a mask, rubber boots, and gloves. I actually didn't use gloves the first few times. To tell you the truth, those times were a bit disturbing.

Talking about disturbing, I have to tell you my most frightening story. It happened when I was exhuming a body not far from here, in fact. When the coffin lid was lifted, everyone was shocked to see the body with its flesh still intact. We had to pour two five-liter bottles of pure alcohol over the body to try to strip off its flesh. And even after all that, I still had to put the bones in a nearby pool of water to rinse them off. After coming home, I couldn't eat, couldn't sleep ... lost a few days because I was so haunted by the vision of what I'd seen. But I still couldn't refuse when the next person came by and asked me to exhume a grave. My wife got really upset at me then, asking me if I wasn't afraid of exhuming again. I kind of just smiled at her [*smiles*]. What else could I do?

People usually exhume bodies at the end of the year when the fields are dry. According to the custom in these parts, we should exhume the body between midnight and 3 a.m., when the winds are quiet and before the sun rises. People don't want to expose human remains to sunlight; that's what Vietnamese people believe, that yin and yang are opposed to one another. The family has to consider all these factors carefully when they're choosing when to exhume the body: if the time is right, then it should be done, no sooner and no later.

I may not be a professional bone cleaner, but I'm pretty good. It's partly because of my experience and partly because I'm careful about what I do. There was a time one winter — it was freezing cold and the rain was drizzling — I came down with the flu right there at the cemetery. But the correct day and time had come. My sense of responsibility meant I just couldn't let the family down. So I dragged myself to the graveside and got the job done. The thing I fear the most are nights when it's rainy and windy: even if I'm wearing a raincoat, I'll still be shivering by the end of it.

These days, people are cremating the dead more and more. I actually hope cremation becomes popular in places like my village, so we can save more land for farming. Cemeteries encroach on scarce farmland and pollute the soil and the groundwater. I'm not worried about being put out of a job; I just hope that we can find ways that the world of the living and the world of the dead can continue to coexist peacefully in the future.

Xuân Canh, November 2011
Michelle Ta, Ngô Mai Hương, Tina Thy Pham, Nguyễn Hà Phương Ninh